HORATIO NELSON

LEADERSHIP ▪ STRATEGY ▪ CONFLICT

ANGUS KONSTAM ▪ ILLUSTRATED BY PETER DENNIS

First published in Great Britain in 2011 by Osprey Publishing,
Midland House, West Way, Botley, Oxford OX2 0PH, UK
44-02 23rd St, Suite 219, Long Island City, NY 11101, USA

E-mail: info@ospreypublishing.com

OSPREY PUBLISHING IS PART OF THE OSPREY GROUP

A CIP catalogue record for this book is available from the British Library.

ISBN: 978 1 84908 495 6

Editorial by Ilios Publishing Ltd, Oxford, UK (www.iliospublishing.com)
Page layout by Myriam Bell Design, France
Index by Michael Forder
Typeset in Stone Serif and Officina Sans
Maps by Mapping Specialists Ltd
Originated by PDQ Digital Media Solutions Ltd, Suffolk
Printed in China through Worldprint Ltd.

11 12 13 14 15   10 9 8 7 6 5 4 3 2 1

Artist's note

Readers may care to note that the original paintings from which the
colour plates in this book were prepared are available for private sale. The
Publishers retain all reproduction copyright whatsoever. All enquiries
should be addressed to:

Peter Dennis, Fieldhead, the Park, Mansfield, NOTTS, NG18 2AT, UK

The Publishers regret that they can enter into no correspondence upon
this matter.

Author's note

Unless otherwise noted, all distances are given in nautical miles
(2,000 yards, or 1,852m), the equivalent of 1.15 land miles, or 1.85km.

All the images are from the author's collection.

Front cover image

© National Maritime Museum, Greenwich, London

The Woodland Trust

Osprey Publishing are supporting the Woodland Trust, the UK's leading
woodland conservation charity, by funding the dedication of trees.

CONTENTS

INTRODUCTION

When the author first joined the Navy the Royal Naval College in Dartmouth was divided into a number of 'houses', just like a public school, only they were called 'divisions'. Midshipman Konstam was assigned to Jellicoe Division, the others being Blake, Hawke, St Vincent and Cunningham. When he asked why there was no Nelson Division, the answer was that it would be grossly unfair to raise one division above all the others. Even then, some 173 years after his death, Nelson was seen as an admiral apart – a naval commander who stood head and shoulders above his peers.

Did Nelson deserve this accolade? Were his undoubted achievements worthy enough for him to be so greatly revered two centuries later? After all, he only fought four fleet actions, and at two of them he served under the command of another admiral. By contrast the other iconic leaders of the age seemed to do much more. Wellington won eight major battles, while Napoleon Bonaparte, self-styled emperor of France fought over two-dozen, most but not all of which were victories. The difference of course is that of the three leaders, Nelson alone understood the importance of sea power. He was without equal in his own martial arena. Napoleon Bonaparte never understood the strategic importance of the fleets he inherited, and consequently he failed to use them effectively. By contrast, Nelson had an innate ability to grasp naval strategy, and he dramatically transformed naval tactics. He became the most effective guarantor of victory in the age of fighting sail.

Nelson, of course, had his faults. He was vain, eccentric, pompous and self-centred. He almost ruined his career through an unseemly affair with a married woman, and for a year he put his personal life ahead of his duty as a naval officer. Unlike many

At the start of the battle of Trafalgar, at around 11.50am, Nelson hoisted his famous signal 'England expects that every man will do his duty.' He originally planned to use the word 'confides' rather than 'expects', but was persuaded to change it by the signal officer, as 'expects' only required one flag rather than several.

of his predecessors he never excelled at naval administration, and never held a position of authority at the Admiralty. He performed no great feats of navigation or seamanship, he never circumnavigated the globe, and he never had to struggle with new technologies like those who came after him. Still, in the naval pantheon he ranks above the Blakes, Hawkes, Jellicoes and Cunninghams, and he eclipses his own superior, the Earl of St Vincent. Even today, Horatio Nelson is the ultimate naval hero of 'immortal memory', a leader whose genius for naval warfare is unquestioned.

Nelson falls to the deck of the *Victory*, watched by a horrified Captain Hardy, in this detail from a copy of *The fall of Nelson, Battle of Trafalgar* by Denis Dighton. Beside him, marines return the fire of the French sharpshooter.

To some he seemed full of bravado, and suffused with an unshakeable belief in his own abilities. He was also a gifted leader of men, and he inspired his captains, his 'band of brothers', to great feats. This though wasn't the root of Nelson's true genius. His gift was that he had a vision of naval warfare that was revolutionary for its time. It was one that rejected the gambit of accepted tactics, of limited naval strategies and the constricting safety of the line of battle. Nelson was the first naval commander of the age of sail to embrace the concept of total war. He not only sought to defeat the enemy, but his objective was to destroy him completely, to remove his ability to wage naval warfare. This is what makes him a great commander.

THE YOUNG NELSON

Had it not been for the death of Nelson's mother there might never have been Lord Nelson, a Trafalgar or an 'immortal memory'. Catherine Nelson was the sister of Maurice Suckling, a successful naval captain. At first there was never any talk of sending her son to sea. Horatio, born on 29 September 1758, was the fourth surviving child of her marriage to the Reverend Edmund Nelson, the rector of Burnham Thorpe in Norfolk. Although a slight, sickly child young Horatio prospered and was schooled in Norfolk. When Catherine died during the Christmas of 1767 her devastated husband was left to raise their eight young children on his own. Captain Suckling attended the funeral, and it was probably there that the idea of a naval career was first mentioned.

In early 1771 the 12-year-old Horatio was sent to serve on board Suckling's ship HMS *Raisonnable* (64 guns), where it was hoped he would take to this harsh new life. Suckling had his doubts, as he thought Horatio was too weak to survive the rough-and-tumble life on board a man-of-war. In March 1771 he joined the ship in the river Medway, rated as a midshipman. When Suckling transferred to the Thames guardship *Triumph* Horatio followed him, and he soon began to settle in, showing a skill for small boat work, navigation and leadership.

As the *Triumph* was a static command, Suckling sent Nelson to sea on board a merchant ship, bound for the West Indies. This insight into nautical life outside the Royal Navy would prove useful, and Nelson gained experience of practical seamanship. This experiment was repeated in 1773 when the 14-year-old joined an expedition to the Arctic, serving as the captain's coxswain on board the exploration ship and former bomb vessel HMS *Carcass*. Once again, Nelson returned that October with valuable experience, and glowing reports. These helped secure him a midshipman's berth on board the frigate HMS *Seahorse* (24), during a cruise to the Persian Gulf and the East Indies. He spent two years on board until laid low by malaria during the summer of 1776. He was sent home to recover, and it was on this miserable voyage that he had a revelation – a quasi-spiritual experience that convinced the teenager that he was destined for greatness. While this can be dismissed as a hallucinatory side effect of his fever, Nelson remained convinced of the event's importance, and consequently of his own destiny.

By the time he reached Britain in September 1776 Nelson had recovered from his illness, and had developed into a rounded, experienced youngster, more than suited for the challenge of a naval career. Thanks to the influence of his uncle he was given a temporary promotion, becoming an acting lieutenant on board HMS *Worcester* (64), then fitting out in Portsmouth for convoy duties in the North Sea, protecting shipping from rebel American privateers. This gave him the experience he needed to sit his lieutenant's examination, which he passed in April 1777. The following day he was appointed to the frigate HMS *Lowestoffe* (32), which was bound for the West Indies, under the command of Captain William Locker. The captain took to his new second lieutenant, and when the *Lowestoffe* captured an American schooner Locker renamed her *Little Lucy* after his daughter, and gave Nelson command of her.

He proved an able commander, and when Locker was invalided home the following summer, he made sure his protégé was transferred to HMS *Bristol* (50), flagship of Admiral Sir Peter Parker. By then France had entered the war, and prizes were to be had aplenty. In December Nelson was given command of one of these prizes, a 12-gun brig which had just been taken into service as HMS *Badger*. As a 'master and commander', Nelson enjoyed the freedom of independent command. It was a necessary first step on the ladder of promotion. His uncle had died in July, and Nelson now had to forge his own career through merit rather than patronage.

Nelson goes to sea, as depicted in a sentimental and inaccurate Victorian scene. In fact his mother died more than three years before he first went to sea in March 1771.

Nelson leaves home to go to Sea for the first time. 1771

Clearly his performance met the approval of his superiors, as in July 1779 Parker promoted him to the rank of post captain. The captain of the frigate HMS *Hinchinbrooke* (28) had just died, and the admiral saw Nelson as his ideal replacement. Spain had now joined the ranks of Britain's enemies, and the Caribbean had become an important theatre of war. For the 20-year-old Nelson, one of the youngest captains in the Navy, the future must have looked very bright indeed.

CAPTAIN NELSON

This promising career almost came to an end less than a year later. In February 1780 an expedition was sent from Jamaica to Nicaragua, to capture a Spanish fortress there. This was meant to sever Spanish communications in Central America and form the basis for a permanent British colony. The *Hinchinbrooke* escorted the troopships to the mouth of the San Juan River, and Nelson, as commander of its naval contingent, then accompanied the force as it moved inland. The Fortress of the Immaculate Conception was besieged on 11 April, and Nelson placed the naval gun batteries whose guns were expected to reduce the stronghold. However, he soon developed dysentery and a fever. Realizing he was likely to die if he remained he had himself rowed downriver to his ship. There he handed over command to Lieutenant Collingwood, who would later act as Nelson's deputy at Trafalgar. Nelson returned to Jamaica, and by September he was back in Britain.

The young Captain Horatio Nelson, an engraving based on the portrait by John Francis Rigaud, which was begun in 1777 when Nelson was a lieutenant, but only completed in 1782, after Nelson's return to Britain from the West Indies.

Nelson had nearly died in the jungles of Nicaragua – most of his men succumbed before the fortress was eventually captured, and then abandoned. He convalesced in Bath, but remained weak and feared that he might never be given another command. He was fortunate to be given the frigate HMS *Albemarle* (28), after the intercession of Maurice's brother William Suckling, the Deputy Collector of Customs. Nelson assumed command in August 1781, and was employed escorting transatlantic convoys. At one stage he was pursued by a French squadron, but managed to evade them amongst the shoals off the Massachusetts coast. By now he was an experienced, confident young captain, and more importantly he had a new mentor.

In the American station he served under Admiral Lord Hood, and the slim young captain impressed his superior. Nelson also had another taste of combat when, in March 1782, he led a small-scale amphibious attack against the French-held Turk's Island, one of the Turks and Caicos Islands. The assault was repulsed – the first of three failures Nelson would experience during his career, all when leading amphibious landings. Lord Hood was understanding about

In 1787 Nelson married Frances ('Fanny') Nisbet (1761–1831), the widowed daughter of a West Indies plantation owner, and a single parent. She was a devoted wife, but became estranged from her husband after he began his affair with Emma Hamilton.

this failure, and he selected Nelson to receive a royal recruit – Prince William, then a midshipman, but later the future King William IV. The prince described his first impression: 'There was something irresistibly pleasing about his address and conversation, and an enthusiasm for professional subjects, that showed he was no common being.' It was the start of an association that would cause trouble for Nelson later in his career.

The war ended in January 1783, and the *Albemarle* was paid off seven months later. He spent the next few months in France, and then returned to Norfolk, where he worried about his prospects of being given another command. This came soon, as in March 1784 he was given HMS *Boreas* (28), a commission which was probably granted following a favourable recommendation by Lord Hood. He was sent to the West Indies with orders to enforce the new Navigation Acts, which excluded American ships from commerce with British-owned ports in the region. This proved a tough law to enforce, as the islanders opposed the act and did what they could to prevent Nelson from implementing it. The only development that alleviated this tiresome duty was a romance with a widow, Frances 'Fanny' Nisbet, the daughter of a Nevis plantation owner. The couple were married on the islands in March 1787, and Prince William, now a naval captain in his own right, took part in the ceremony.

That summer the *Boreas* returned to Britain, and in November she was paid off. Nelson took his new wife back to his father's rectory in Burnham Thorpe, where he lived on half pay while waiting for another command. His zealous performance in the West Indies had done little to increase his standing in the Admiralty – quite the reverse. Lord Hood was now reluctant to help him, and Nelson began to resign himself to the prospect of a frugal rural existence in Norfolk. Even this was threatened by lawsuits emanating from his seizure of American ships in the West Indies.

It was a frustrating time for Nelson. He occupied himself with reading, studying current affairs, landscaping the rectory garden and playing his part in Norfolk society. In short, he spent his years ashore living the quiet life of a country gentleman, and writing to anyone who might have influence, begging them for a ship. One of the problems was that Nelson had formed too close an association with Prince William, who became the Duke of Clarence in 1789. The prince was a mediocre naval officer, and Nelson's support of him led to his censure by King George III. This tied the hands of Lord Hood and Lord Howe, who might otherwise have used their influence to help him.

What saved Nelson from obscurity was the threat of a new war. In 1789 France erupted in bloody revolution. While there was no immediate prospect of war, the fleet was mobilized in 1790, ostensibly to counter the threat of a war with Spain. Nelson was still left without a ship, but as the political climate deteriorated it became increasingly likely that Britain might find herself at war with Revolutionary France. In June 1791 the French royal family tried to flee the country, but were captured and returned to Paris. The following summer the mob stormed the Tuileries Palace and the royal couple were arrested. Austria and Prussia declared war on France, and the fledgling French Republic was hard pressed to defend its borders.

Then, in January 1793, Jacobin revolutionaries executed Louis XVI. This proved too much for Britain, who promptly declared war on the French Republic. In late 1792, the Admiralty remembered Captain Nelson, and he was called in to see the Earl of Chatham, First Lord of the Admiralty. Chatham offered Nelson command of a ship-of-the-line, either a 64-gun third rate nearing completion, or a 74-gun ship if he were prepared to wait a little longer. Nelson opted for the first available ship, which turned out to be HMS *Agamemnon* (64), then refitting in Chatham. Not only had Nelson got his command at last, but it was a prestigious ship-of-the-line, and she would be ready to play her part in the coming war.

Nelson took command of the *Agamemnon* in early February, two days before the declaration of war. He recruited a new volunteer crew for her in Norfolk and Suffolk, augmented by men rounded up by press gangs. She was finally ready for service in April, but she remained in home waters for another two months until Lord Hood was ready to sail for the Mediterranean with 11 ships-of-the-line, which would constitute the Mediterranean Fleet once they reached Gibraltar. The *Agamemnon* sailed with them, and on 22 June the fleet reached Cadiz, where the British officers were entertained by their Spanish counterparts. Nelson thought little of the Spanish fleet there, writing 'They have four First-Rates in commission in Cadiz, and very fine ships, but shockingly manned.' This poor opinion would play a major part in his actions during the battle of St Vincent less than four years later. He was equally unimpressed by a bullfight he was invited to watch – a spectacle he found sickening.

The fleet was reinforced by four more ships-of-the-line at Gibraltar, and by early August it was off Toulon where the French Mediterranean fleet was stationed. All wasn't well in the port, as the inhabitants feared the spread of Jacobin extremism from Paris, and tales of mass executions in nearby Marseilles fuelled this fear. Consequently Toulon declared its allegiance to the late King Louis, and its leading citizens invited Lord Hood into their port. Therefore, on 27 August, the British gained control of the base, and the fleet.

Nelson was sent to Naples to collect reinforcements to aid the port's defence, and it was there that he first met Sir William Hamilton, the British envoy at the Neapolitan court, and his new wife Emma. Lady Hamilton made a favourable impression on Nelson, but it would be another five years before they began their infamous liaison.

Prince William (1765–1837) was the third son of King George III, who succeeded his brother to the throne in 1833, becoming William IV. Nelson's friendship with the rakish prince was viewed with suspicion by both the court and the Admiralty.

His next mission was to take the *Agamemnon* to Cagliari in Sardinia, and on 22 November Nelson encountered a squadron of French frigates. Nelson gave chase, and overhauled the *Melpomène* (44). However, the *Agamemnon* was heavily outnumbered, and although she crippled the *Melpomène,* the rigging of the British man-of-war was badly damaged and Nelson was forced to break off the action. Still, it showed an aggressive spirit and a willingness to defy numerical odds.

Nelson's birthplace and childhood home, the Rectory at Burnham Thorpe in Norfolk, from an early 19th-century painting. In 1788 Nelson returned here with Fanny, living a frugal existence on half pay.

The *Agamemnon* was repaired in Leghorn, and while she was there Toulon fell to the French, after a spirited siege masterminded by Napoleon Bonaparte, a rising star in the French Army. In January, Nelson was ordered to Corsica to assist the Corsican patriot General de Paoli, who had offered to cede the island to the British if they helped him capture the French garrisons at Bastia, San Fiorenzo and Calvi. Nelson blockaded Bastia, but he also launched small raids on the Corsican mainland. In one he and 60 men captured a flour mill outside San Fiorenzo – the only one in the region. The landing party burned it, and threw the flour into the sea. He also destroyed local shipping, and captured a small fort outside Bastia.

On 19 February a brigade of British troops landed at San Fiorenzo and captured the small town. That left the French garrisons at Bastia and Calvi to deal with. Bastia was already encircled by Corsican insurgents and blockaded by Hood and Nelson. It was hoped that in time hunger would force the garrison to capitulate. To encourage them Nelson landed eight

Captain Nelson at the siege of Calvi, July 1794

From early on in his naval career Nelson developed a style of leadership based on encouragement and example, rather than blind obedience. As a result he frequently led from the front, for example leading a boarding party at St Vincent, a landing party at Tenerife or placing his flagship at the forefront of the line of battle at Trafalgar. This command style was first established during the siege of Calvi, off the northern coast of Corsica. On 20 June 1794 Nelson supervised an amphibious landing by a brigade of British infantry, who set about investing the French-held port. A battery was established more than a mile from the town's defences, but on 6 July an advanced battery was set up just 700 yards (640m) from the French positions. The guns in the battery were 24-pdrs, landed from Nelson's ship HMS *Agamemnon*, and crewed by her men. On 10 July Nelson was directing the fire of the battery, and the French were firing back. Then, soon after 7am, a French roundshot struck the defences, and a shower of stones and sand flew into Nelson's face. He was blinded in his right eye, but true to form he remained at his post and supervised the successful completion of the siege.

After Nelson lost the use of his right eye at the siege of Calvi (1794) he occasionally wore an eyepatch, to protect his damaged eye. However, vanity precluded wearing it in public – it was reserved for use aboard ship.

of the *Agamemnon*'s guns, establishing a battery on the hills overlooking the town. For the next six weeks he acted as an artillery commander, directing the bombardment of the port. In mid-May the British troops in Corsica were reinforced, and arrived to lay siege to the town. By that time the garrison had enough, and they surrendered on 21 May.

The *Agamemnon* was sent to Gibraltar for a refit, and by the time she returned in late June the British were ready to lay siege to Calvi. On 20 June Nelson supervised the landing of a British infantry brigade, and within a fortnight a battery had been built, and was firing at the outer defences of the town. On 6 July an advanced battery was built within 700 yards (640m) of the town's main bastion, Fort Mozzello. Once again, Nelson supplied the guns and crews, and supervised the bombardment. The French defended the little port with vigour, and at dawn on 10 July they opened up a heavy fire on the new battery. At 7am Nelson was hit in the face by a shower of sand and stone thrown up when a French roundshot hit the earthen parapet. He remained at his post, but the injury was a serious one and Nelson lost the use of his right eye. He made light of the injury, and wrote to Fanny saying that it was barely noticeable. Instead, he regarded it as a badge of honour.

Calvi finally surrendered on 10 August 1794, as too did the two French frigates trapped in the harbour, one of which was the *Melpomène*. With the gruelling little Corsican campaign at an end, Nelson had his eye treated by Lord Hood's physician, and then took the *Agamemnon* back to Leghorn for another much-needed refit. Britain now had a secure base within range of Toulon, and when the blockade there was renewed the Mediterranean Fleet was able to maintain a close watch on the French port.

Nelson had played an important part in the Corsican campaign, and he was starting to be noticed. Still, while he had a strong belief in his own destiny, others still had to be convinced that this slight, energetic and somewhat precocious post captain was marked for greatness.

THE YEARS OF DESTINY

In the spring of 1795, Horatio Nelson had been a post captain for more than 15 years, he had gained a wealth of experience and commanded a ship-of-the-line. However, apart from a few minor skirmishes he had never fought in a proper single-ship action, let alone a full-scale sea battle. All of that was about to change. For the next decade he would fight a series of increasingly important fleet battles, rising to the challenges of naval command and revelling in the laurels of victory.

The naval situation, 1793–1805

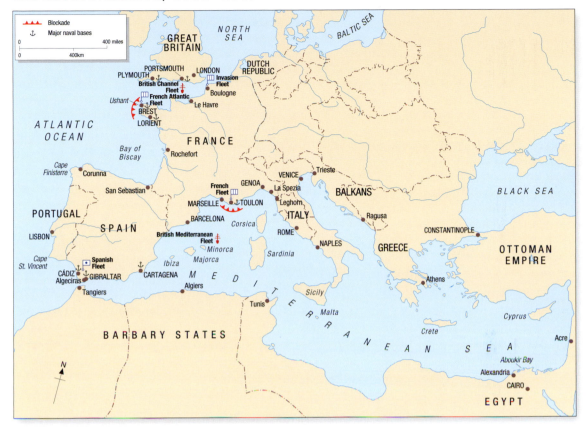

Hotham's action off Genoa, 1795

In October 1794 Vice-Admiral Sir William Hotham replaced Lord Hood as the commander of the Mediterranean Fleet. Hotham was a competent but unimaginative commander and lacked his predecessor's aggression. He maintained the blockade of Toulon throughout the winter, until in March 1795 the French managed to slip past him in bad weather with 15 ships-of-the-line. Contre-Amiral Pierre Martin's fleet was bound for Corsica, escorting an invasion force which planned to reclaim the island from the British.

Hotham set off in pursuit with 14 ships-of-the-line, and the two fleets sighted each other on the morning of 12 March. The French fleet ran back towards Toulon, but the *Ça Ira* (80) lost her topmasts in a collision and lagged behind, allowing the British frigate *Inconstant* (36) to overhaul her. *Inconstant* harried her until Nelson arrived in *Agamemnon* (64). For the next two hours Nelson pounded the *Ça Ira*, which was being towed to safety by a French frigate. The towed ship was unable to reply effectively, and the *Ça Ira* was soon turned into a floating wreck.

Hotham ordered Nelson to withdraw when the *Sans Culottes* (120) appeared, but the British shadowed the French throughout the night and the action began again the following morning. By then the *Ça Ira* was being

13

The capture of the *Ça Ira* by Nelson's 64-gun HMS *Agamemnon* in the Gulf of Genoa on 14 March 1795 earned Nelson his first independent command, and first brought him to the attention of the British public.

towed by *La Censeur* (74). In the battle that followed *La Censeur* lost her mainmast, and *Ça Ira* was completely dismasted. Both ships struck their colours soon afterwards.

Hotham was happy with the outcome, writing 'We must be contented – we have done very well.' This wasn't good enough for Nelson. He wrote to Fanny: 'Had we taken ten sail, and allowed the eleventh to escape… I could never call it well done.' He wanted to destroy the enemy, not merely harm him.

Despite or possibly because of his outburst, Hotham decided to give Nelson an independent command, and for the next few months the *Agamemnon* harried the Riviera coast. In June the French fleet pursued him, but, although Nelson lured them towards Hotham's fleet, the Admiral's response was half hearted and all but one of the French ships returned to port safely.

Nelson took out his frustration on a French convoy, which he captured near Genoa, and on the coastal shipping of the French Riviera, which he forced into port. In December the lacklustre Hotham was replaced by Sir John Jervis, an inspiring commander who Nelson respected. The political situation was deteriorating for the Allies, and the fast-changing situation would test both Jervis and Nelson, and give them the chance to display their skill.

The battle of Cape St Vincent, 1797

Admiral Jervis recognized talent when he saw it, and gave Nelson the temporary rank of commodore, allowing him to continue his independent command. In March 1796 General Bonaparte assumed command of the French Army of Italy, and a month later he launched a whirlwind campaign that forced Piedmont-Sardinia out of the war and drove the Austrians back across Northern Italy as far as Mantua. In June the French captured Leghorn, which the Royal Navy had been using as a base, and it became clear that the Allies might be driven out of Italy altogether.

Then, in August, France and Spain signed the Treaty of Ildefonso, and the Spanish became French allies. A formal declaration of war followed in October, thereby doubling the size of the fleet ranged against Britain. This also raised the spectre of a joint Franco-Spanish fleet spearheading an invasion of Britain. Consequently the Mediterranean Fleet had to be ready to intervene, and so it was withdrawn to Gibraltar and then Lisbon. The British Government was forced to abandon its remaining Italian allies for the time being.

This meant that Corsica had to be abandoned, and, with the exception of Elba, the Western Mediterranean effectively became the exclusive preserve of the French and Spanish. Jervis had to be content with blockading Cadiz, and preventing the enemy from breaking out into the Atlantic Ocean. In fact Cadiz was largely empty, and the bulk of the French Mediterranean Fleet had already slipped out into the Atlantic in mid-December as part of an ultimately unsuccessful French attempt to invade Ireland.

By the start of 1797 it was clear that the Spanish Fleet gathered at Cartagena was planning to put to sea. Jervis brought the Mediterranean Fleet round to Cape St Vincent, on the south-western tip of Portugal, and awaited developments.

Nelson rejoined the fleet on 13 February, after passing the Spanish fleet off Cadiz the day before. He reported that he had looked in to both Toulon and Cartagena, but had seen no sign of the enemy. It was now apparent that the French had gone, and the Spanish were mounting an operation of their own. This involved the escort of a convoy from Malaga to Cadiz, a move that involved passing through the Straits of Gibraltar and risking an encounter with Jervis' fleet. Therefore the new Spanish commander, Teniente-General (Admiral) José Córdoba y Ramos, decided to use his entire fleet to escort the convoy. He hoped to intimidate Jervis by sheer numbers, and so reach Cadiz without being attacked.

Córdoba underestimated the resolve of Jervis, and the vagaries of the weather. On 6 February he was within sight of Cadiz when an easterly gale sprang up, and the Spanish headed west into the Atlantic to ride out the storm. It finally blew itself out on 12 February, and the battered fleet tried its best to regroup and then set a course for Cadiz. This was when Nelson spotted them, on his way to the Cape St Vincent rendezvous. The two fleets were now only a few miles apart.

At dawn broke on 14 February – St Valentine's Day – the Spanish fleet lay about 35 miles to the south-west of Cape St Vincent, with 27 ships-of-the-line. Jervis and his 15 ships-of-the-line were 10 miles to the north. The weather was fair, with a light breeze from the west-south-west, with a low mist obscuring visibility. Both sides knew the other fleet was there, and so Córdoba altered course to the south-east, away from the potential threat.

At 10am the mist thinned enough for the two fleets to sight each other. Jervis now knew that the Spanish outnumbered him by nearly two to one. The two fleets were now on converging courses, with the Spanish slightly ahead of the British. It was at this point that Córdoba realized that his rearmost division was in danger of being caught and destroyed before the rest of the fleet could support it. He therefore ordered a change of course, with all flagships turning

Commodore Nelson in HMS *Captain*, pictured approaching the Spanish second rate *San Nicolas*, with the first rate *San José* behind her. Nelson's spectacular capture of the two ships turned the battle of Cape St Vincent (1797) from a stalemate into a British victory.

15

simultaneously to the north, followed by the rest of their divisions. The result was the collapse of any formation.

Córdoba was correct – Jervis planned to cut the Spanish line and isolate the rearmost enemy division. The Spanish change of course did little to alter his plan – only now the gap he was heading for lay between the leading Spanish division and the one in the centre. Effectively, the leading Spanish division – the van – under the command of Vicealmirante (Vice-Admiral) Moreno had become the rearguard, and the rear, under Vicealmirante Morales de los Rios, was now the van. Jervis was heading straight for the gap between Moreno's division and the main body of the fleet, where Córdoba flew his flag in the *Santisima Trinidad* (130).

It was a race. Just before noon the leading British ship *Culloden* (74) was abreast of the *Santisima Trinidad*, heading towards Moreno's flagship the *Principe de Asturias* (112). Moreno veered to port, and the two ships exchanged broadsides – the opening shots of the battle. The *Principe de Asturias* fell away, and the *Culloden* swept through the gap she left, followed by the *Blenheim* (98) and Vice-Admiral Parker in the *Prince George* (98), with the *Orion* (74) close astern of her. By noon, Jervis had cut the Spanish fleet in two. Ignoring Moreno's isolated division, he ordered the *Culloden* to head north, followed in succession by the rest of the fleet, maintaining a neat line of battle.

By 12.50pm the British and Spanish fleets were in three distinct groups: the main Spanish fleet to the north was still heading away from the action; Moreno's division was still to the south; the British ships lay between them, deployed in a large 'U' shape. Nelson had been watching the battle unfold from the quarterdeck of his new command, HMS *Captain* (74). Nelson's ship was fourth from the end of the line, and it was now apparent that if he followed orders, Córdoba and his fleet would manage to escape. Ahead of him in the line were two senior officers – Vice-Admiral Thompson in the *Britannia* (100) and Vice-Admiral Waldegrave in the *Barfleur* (98). Neither of the two admirals appeared concerned, and they continued to obey their orders to the letter.

Fortunately Nelson was made of sterner stuff. He didn't hesitate. He turned the *Captain* to port, and pulled out of the line, leaving a gap between the *Barfleur* ahead and the *Namur* (90) astern of him. Nelson wore around in a circle making a 270-degree turn, and he cut through the line of ships behind him, passing between the *Diadem* (64) and the *Excellent* (74). He headed straight for the right flank of the Spanish fleet, and was therefore the only ship able to support the *Culloden* as it bore up from the south. The time was about 1pm. It was the defining moment of the battle.

On board the *Victory*, Captain Calder asked Jervis if he should send a signal to recall Nelson. The Admiral

The largest warship of the age of sail was the Spanish first rate *Santisima Trinidad*, which carried 136 guns, mounted on four gundecks. At St Vincent and Trafalgar she proved lumbering and ungainly. Almost captured in 1797, she finally surrendered in 1805.

The battle of Cape St Vincent, 14 February 1797

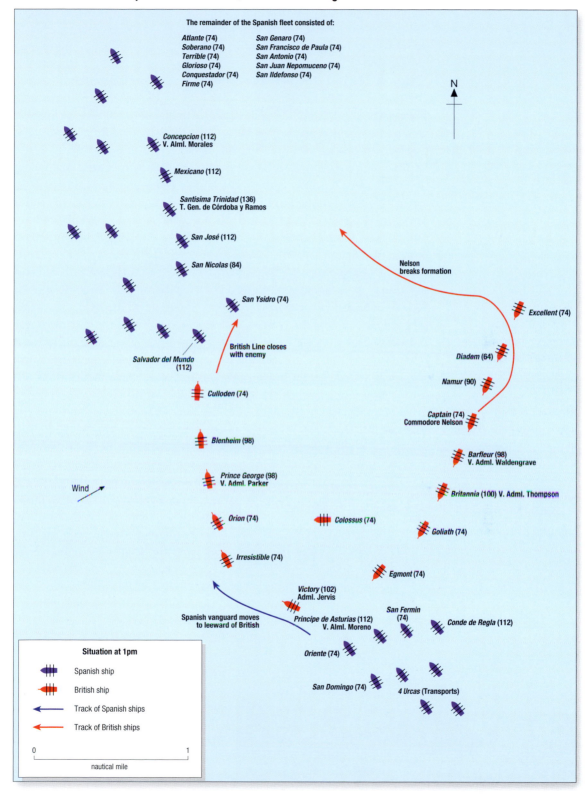

The remainder of the Spanish fleet consisted of:

Atlante (74)   San Genaro (74)
Soberano (74)   San Francisco de Paula (74)
Terrible (74)   San Antonio (74)
Glorioso (74)   San Juan Nepomuceno (74)
Conquestador (74)   San Ildefonso (74)
Firme (74)

N

Concepcion (112)
V. Alml. Morales

Mexicano (112)

Santisima Trinidad (136)
T. Gen. de Córdoba y Ramos

San José (112)

San Nicolas (84)

San Ysidro (74)

Nelson
breaks formation

Excellent (74)

Salvador del Mundo
(112)

British Line closes
with enemy

Diadem (64)

Culloden (74)

Namur (90)

Captain (74)
Commodore Nelson

Blenheim (98)

Barfleur (98)
V. Adml. Waldengrave

Prince George (98)
V. Adml. Parker

Wind

Britannia (100) V. Adml. Thompson

Orion (74)

Colossus (74)

Goliath (74)

Irresistible (74)

Egmont (74)

Victory (102)
Adml. Jervis

San Fermin
(74)

Conde de Regla (112)

Spanish vanguard moves
to leeward of British

Principe de Asturias (112)
V. Alml. Moreno

Oriente (74)

San Domingo (74)

4 Urcas (Transports)

Situation at 1pm

Spanish ship

British ship

Track of Spanish ships

Track of British ships

0   1

nautical mile

refused, and ordered the rest of the fleet to break formation and to sail in support. Some historians described Nelson's action as disobedient. Instead, he had a better idea of his admiral's wishes than other more senior officers in the fleet. By 1.20pm the flagship was flying Signal 16, 'Engage the enemy more closely'.

Nelson set a course to intercept Córdoba's flagship the *Santisima Trinidad*. The *Culloden* was simultaneously approaching the rear of the huddle of Spanish ships, and Troubridge altered course to starboard, skirting the Spanish fleet so he could support Nelson. By this stage other British ships were breaking away to intercept the Spanish, led by the *Excellent* at the rear of the British line. Against a well-drilled fleet Nelson's action would have been suicidal. Instead it simply exposed the terrible shortcomings of the Spanish.

The *Captain* found herself ranged against the *San Nicolas* (84) and *San José* (112). The *Culloden* arrived too, and, while the *Captain* split her fire, the *Culloden* astern of her concentrated on the *San José*. After about ten minutes the rigging of the *Culloden* was hit and she fell away, leaving both Spanish ships to concentrate on the *Captain*. Nelson was outnumbered and outgunned, but Captain Collingwood of the *Excellent* appeared and averted disaster by sailing his ship between the Spaniards and Nelson. The *Excellent* ranged alongside the *San Nicolas*, which veered to windward to thwart any boarding attempt. Collingwood's ship edged ahead a little, but at that moment a shot from the *Captain* brought down the mizzenmast of the *San José*, and she veered to leeward. The two Spanish ships collided, and became locked together by their tangle of fallen sails.

The *Captain* was badly damaged, her sails were shot through and the ship's wheel shattered. Before she lost steerage way completely Nelson ordered Captain Miller to put the helm over, bringing her alongside the starboard quarter of the *San Nicolas*. Nelson led the boarding party that clambered on board the Spanish second rate. On the *Captain* a detachment of the 69th (South Lincolnshire) Foot were standing in for the Royal Marines, and so soldiers spearheaded Nelson's attack. In his own account of the action Nelson gave full credit to these men:

The soldiers of the 69th Regiment with an alacrity that will ever do them credit, and Lieutenant Pearson of the same regiment, were among the foremost in this service. The first man who jumped into the enemy's mizzen chains was Captain Berry, late my First Lieutenant.... A soldier of the 69th regiment having broke the upper quarter-gallery window jumped in, followed by myself and others as fast

Commodore Nelson boarding the Spanish first rate *San José*, during the battle of Cape St Vincent (1797), based on an original painting by George Jones. The capture of two large enemy ships in this dramatic manner made Nelson a household name.

as possible.... Having pushed on to the quarterdeck I found Captain Berry in possession of the poop, and the Spanish ensign hauling down.

Nelson was now in possession of the *San Nicolas*. However, he and his men were now coming under fire from the first rate *San José*, which lay alongside the port beam of the *San Nicolas*. Nelson saw little option but to continue the fight. He led his men up onto the deck of the *San José*. The Spanish promptly surrendered, and, as Nelson put it, 'It was not long until I was on the quarterdeck, when the Spanish captain, with a bow, presented me his sword, and said the Admiral [Contra-almirante (Rear-Admiral) Don Xavier Winthuysen] was dying of his wounds below.'

Nelson collected the swords of the Spanish officers, and passed them to his bargeman William Fearney, who bundled them under his arm. This spirited boarding action caught the imagination of both the fleet and the British public, and the advance from one ship to the other was later described as 'Nelson's patent bridge for boarding First Rates'.

Admiral John Jervis (1735–1823), who became the Earl of St Vincent after his victory in 1797, was known as a strict disciplinarian, but he also recognized Nelson's talents, and approved of his dramatic use of his own initiative at the battle of Cape St Vincent

While Nelson secured his two prizes, the last stages of the battle played themselves out. Ahead of the three interlocked ships Córdoba bravely placed his flagship between the British ships and the rest of his fleet. Over the next 90 minutes the huge Spanish ship was badly battered, but she fought on until 4.20pm when Jervis ordered his ships to break off the action. Astern of Nelson, Jervis in the *Victory* had overhauled the *Salvador del Mundo* (112), which surrendered after another lengthy duel. Finding herself cut off and unable to rejoin the rest of the fleet, the *San Ysidro* (74) also surrendered.

The two fleets separated, leaving the British with four prizes. After the battle, when Nelson went aboard the *Victory* Jervis embraced him, and thanked the commodore for using his initiative. When Captain Calder reminded the Admiral that Nelson had disobeyed his orders, Jervis said to Nelson 'It certainly was so, and if you commit such a breach [again] I will forgive you also.'

That day the frigate *Lively* was sent to Britain with Jervis' despatches, and when news of his victory was made public Nelson became the hero of the hour. On board the *Lively* was Sir Gilbert Elliot, former British viceroy of Corsica and a good friend of Nelson. Before she sailed, the commodore had a word with Sir Gilbert's aide, and told him that if he was to be rewarded for his actions, he preferred the Order of the Bath to the award of a baronetcy. He wanted a decoration he could wear rather than a title he could not. Few things better demonstrate the two sides of Nelson than this – the spirited naval commander whose actions turned the tide of a battle, and the vain seeker of adulation concerned with the visible trappings of success.

In the end Nelson had his way. Not only was he made a Knight Companion of the Order of the Bath (KB), but he was also promoted to Rear-Admiral. Just as importantly to Nelson, he had become a household name and was widely commended for both his bravery and his tactical abilities. The battle of Cape St Vincent was a real turning point for Nelson. From that moment on, his star was in the ascendant.

Tenerife, 1797

After his victory, Admiral Jervis became the Earl St Vincent, but he remained off Cadiz, keeping the Spanish bottled up in port. Nelson also remained with the fleet, but he and Captain Miller were transferred from the *Captain* to the *Theseus* (74), whose crew were suspected of being on the verge of mutiny. Instead he was handed an anonymous note, claiming that the crew were happy to serve under him. Nelson not only knew how to inspire his officers, but his men were also willing to follow him anywhere. Still, blockading an enemy port was dull work, and Nelson spiced things up by participating in a raid on the harbour – using a bomb ketch to shell the port, then personally heading off a counterattack by Spanish gunboats by attacking them using longboats. At one stage Nelson and the crew of his longboat were almost overwhelmed, but the admiral was saved by the arrival of reinforcements.

The blockade continued, but the Spanish refused to come out and give battle. In April Nelson proposed launching an attack on Santa Cruz, the main port on Tenerife in the Spanish-owned Canary Islands. The port was a stopping off place for Spanish treasure ships, and word reached the British that the treasure ship *San José* was in the port carrying a valuable cargo of silver from the New World. Nelson was ordered to take a small squadron and assault the town.

The wounding of Rear-Admiral Nelson, just as he was about to disembark onto the Spanish-held mole at Santa Cruz de Tenerife, is depicted in a stirring but unrealistically melodramatic style in this copy of an original painting by Richard Westall.

Nelson was detached from the fleet with eight ships – the third rates *Theseus*, *Culloden* and *Zealous*, the frigates *Seahorse*, *Emerald* and *Terpsichore*, plus the cutter *Fox* and the mortar boat *Terror*. He knew little about the defences of Tenerife, save that around 3,000 men garrisoned it, under the command of Commandant-General Don Antonio Gutierrez. Santa Cruz was a difficult place to attack. Steep mountains flanked the port, and the rocky coast lacked good landing places. The port itself was guarded by three forts and nine batteries, linked by a stone wall that served as a breastwork. Nelson initially rejected the idea of a frontal attack. Instead he planned to use the advantage of surprise and launch a night attack against the northern end of the port's defences. Once lodged ashore he could land guns to pound the town into submission.

Nelson reached Tenerife on 15 July, by which time the assault was meticulously planned. Bad weather delayed the operation for a week, and the flotilla stood out to sea until the weather eased. The assault finally went in on the night of 22–23 July. Captain Troubridge of the *Culloden* led the force of 1,000 sailors and marines, embarked in the flotilla's small boats. Frigates towed these boats to within a mile of the shore, where they were cast loose.

When Nelson arrived off Tenerife at dawn on 23 July he was horrified to see that the boats had still not reached the beach. A strong offshore wind had sprung up, and progress had slowed to a crawl. The element of surprise was lost, and so Troubridge called off the attack. Nelson had no option but to withdraw. He and Troubridge improvised another landing at the mouth of the Bufadero, a stream 3 land miles (5km) to the north-east of the town. The landing was successful, but between the beach and the town lay a steep hill, which was climbed in the midday heat. On reaching the summit they found another ridge barring their way. Troubridge withdrew, as his men were suffering badly from heatstroke and thirst.

That evening, Nelson made the worst decision of his career. He decided to launch another attack, and this time he would make a frontal assault on the town itself. While this seemed suicidal, he was buoyed by the report of a prisoner that the Spanish defenders lacked the will to resist. He laid plans for a night attack, where everything would depend on speed, determination and luck. He was driven by a sense of frustration and the prospect of failure. This time, though, Nelson would lead the assault himself.

The plan called for the 1,000-strong force in six groups to land on the mole in front of the town square, now the Plaza Candelaria. After re-forming they would assault the adjacent Castillo de San Cristóbal, the key to the town's defences. On 24 April the frigates towed the longboats to within 2 miles of the town, and, at 10.30pm the boats were cast off and began their long row inshore. The cutter *Fox* was towed behind the boats, carrying a floating reserve of 200 men. The approach took over two hours, but by 1am the ships were within sight of the mole.

That was when it all went wrong. A Spanish sentry spotted the boats and raised the alarm. Batteries lining the waterfront began firing, and small-arms fire erupted from the sea wall. As Nelson put it, 'Unfortunately the greatest part of the boats did not see the mole, but went on shore through a raging surf, which stove all the boats to the left of it.' In fact the current had carried most of the boats to the south, and the men were forced to struggle ashore

During the Battle of Cape St Vincent (1797) the Spanish fleet lost any organized formation after Admiral Jervis' fleet divided it in two. In this view of the battle, Jervis' flagship *Victory* passes astern of the Spanish first rate *Salvador del Mundo*.

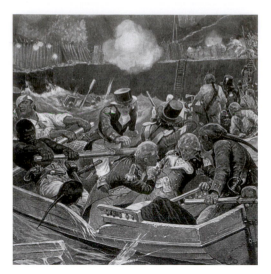

During the abortive amphibious assault at Santa Cruz de Tenerife on 24 July 1797, Nelson was hit in the right arm by a musket ball, a wound that led to the loss of his limb. His life was saved by his stepson, who whipped a tourniquet around Nelson's arm.

wherever they could. At the base of the mole Captain Bowen of the *Terpishore* overran a gun battery, but found himself pinned down by heavy fire from the Castillo. Things quickly began to unravel.

Nelson was just about to land on the mole when a musket ball struck him on the right arm just above the elbow, and he collapsed back into the boat. Fortunately, his quick-thinking stepson Lieutenant Josiah Nesbit whipped a tourniquet around Nelson's arm and ordered an undamaged boat to take the admiral back to his flagship. Meanwhile the attack was faltering. The whole assault force was pinned down along 300 yards (270m) of the waterfront. By this time the *Fox* had been sunk, some 300 yards (270m) from the shore.

Captain Troubridge now took command and tried to bluff Gutierrez into surrendering. The Spanish commander was having none of it. Troubridge realized he had to get his men moving, so he led them into the town where they found themselves surrounded and forced to barricade themselves inside a convent.

Back on the seafront Captain Hood of the *Zealous* organized a truce, which allowed him to send the wounded back to the ships. On the *Theseus* the ship's surgeon examined Nelson's shattered arm, and decided that there was no alternative but to amputate. Nelson endured the operation with great stoicism, and an hour later he was back on deck as dawn revealed the full extent of the disaster.

At 7am the garrison in the convent surrendered, and they were given leave to return to their ships. Nelson watched his men return, and then retired to his cabin to write his report to Jervis using his left hand. It was clear that his injury caused Nelson to despair of ever seeing action again. In his jerkily penned covering letter to Jervis he wrote, 'I have become a burden to my friends and useless to my country… I become dead to the world – I go hence and am no more seen… I hope you will be able to give me a frigate to convey the remains of my carcass to England.' He finished by adding; 'You will excuse my scrawl, considering it is my first attempt.'

The convalescent

The voyage back to Cadiz took three weeks, during which Nelson despaired for the future. St Vincent was very supportive, saying that Nelson and his men had displayed 'the greatest heroism and perseverance'. Nelson was sent home, accompanied by the other wounded officers. Before he left, St Vincent acceded to Nelson's wishes and promoted Lieutenant Nesbit to master and commander. He was later given command of the *Dolphin* (24), the start of a short and undistinguished naval career.

Back home in Britain Josiah's mother Fanny had to learn to dress Nelson's wound. His health slowly improved, although he remained in great pain until December when the ligatures were finally removed. Much of his convalescence was spent in Bath, and Nelson received numerous letters of sympathy. The king received him at Court during his investiture as a Knight Companion, and other honours followed, including the freedom of both Norwich and London. Best of all though, the Admiralty promised him a new command.

Nelson was offered the *Foudroyant* (80), which was then being built in Plymouth, but as he was recovering faster than expected he told the Admiralty that he preferred a ship that was already in service. He was given the *Vanguard* (74), refitting in Portsmouth. The country certainly needed him. After the spectacular successes of General Bonaparte in Italy, Austria sued for peace, leaving Britain to face France, Holland and Spain on her own. The naval situation improved slightly in October when Admiral Duncan defeated the Dutch at the battle of Camperdown. Nevertheless, the Mediterranean was now a French lake, and the threat of a cross-Channel invasion remained very real.

On 29 March 1798 Nelson hoisted his flag on the *Vanguard*. His orders were to join St Vincent off Cadiz, and with his help the fleet there was expected to reclaim the Mediterranean from the French. It was long overdue – all winter a re-formed French Fleet had been fitting out in Toulon, while a transport fleet was being assembled. The French were obviously planning a major operation.

The *Vanguard* rendezvoused with the Mediterranean Fleet on 30 April. Nelson was given command of a flotilla consisting of the third rates *Vanguard*, *Orion* and *Alexander* and three frigates. His orders were to discover exactly what was going on in Toulon. His presence in the Mediterranean was also meant to bolster the morale of Austria, and Britain's remaining supporters in Italy.

The battle of the Nile, 1798

Nelson sailed from Gibraltar on 8 May, and 12 days later his flotilla was in the Gulf of Lyon. There he encountered a severe storm, and the *Vanguard* was nearly wrecked on the coast of Sardinia. This storm couldn't have been more fortuitous for the French. As Nelson and his force were being battered by the gale, a French invasion force of 13 ships-of-the-line, 31 frigates and sloops, and 280 transports slipped out of Toulon and headed out into the Mediterranean, passing to the east of Corsica. On board the transports were 36,500 veteran French troops, led by

A graphic depiction of the explosion of the French flagship *L'Orient* at the battle of the Nile, a disaster that came to symbolize the decisive victory achieved by Nelson off the Egyptian coast in August 1798.

the same General Bonaparte who had driven the Austrians from Italy. Unbeknown to the British, his army had been dubbed 'The Army of the Orient', and his expedition was bound for Egypt.

On 24 May St Vincent sent Nelson reinforcements: ten 74-gun third rates, a fifth rate of 50 guns and a frigate, all under the command of Captain Troubridge. Nelson now commanded an impressive force of 14 ships-of-the-line; the third rates *Alexander, Audacious, Bellerophon, Culloden, Defence, Goliath, Majestic, Minotaur, Orion, Swiftsure, Theseus, Vanguard* and *Zealous,* as well as the fourth rate *Leander.* For the first time Nelson was in command of an entire fleet of powerful ships-of-the-line, crewed by highly experienced men. All he needed to do now was to encounter the French.

When he reached Toulon he discovered the port was empty. He was sure the French were heading south towards Italy, Sicily or the Eastern Mediterranean. He set off in pursuit, reaching Naples on 15 June, but without sighting the enemy. In fact, Bonaparte and his naval commander Vice-Amiral (Vice-Admiral) Brueys were at Malta, which Bonaparte attacked and captured after a token resistance by the Knights of St John.

When Nelson finally learned where the French were he raced south through the Straits of Messina between Sicily and the Italian mainland. The French left Malta on 19 June, and a passing ship brought Nelson word that Malta had fallen and that the French were at sea again. Nelson hoped to intercept Brueys somewhere to the east of Malta. Instead, on the night of 22–23 June the two fleets passed within a few miles of each other, each fleet

The poop deck of HMS *Vanguard* at the battle of the Nile, August 1798

When Rear-Admiral Nelson caught up with the Vice-Amiral Bruey's French Fleet at Aboukir Bay on the evening of 1 August, he was able to launch an immediate attack, because he had already briefed his captains and they knew exactly what was expected of them. They already understood Nelson's desire to concentrate their forces against part of the enemy fleet – the only decision Nelson had to make was which part of the enemy formation he should attack. Brueys had conveniently anchored his ships in a line, and imagined they were protected by shallow water on their landward side. Nelson made four signals during the approach. The first was to 'engage the enemy centre' and 'engage the enemy van', which told his captains where to direct the attack. Then came 'form line as most convenient'. This told them to disregard the conventional line of battle, but to select their own opponents, which was followed by 'make all sail', the signal to commence the attack. In this scene Nelson (1) is looking astern, towards the seven British ships behind him, as the *Vanguard* bears down on the centre of the French line. The French are already firing at the oncoming ships, but like the others the *Vanguard* is reserving her fire until she gets within point-blank range. The signals midshipman and the yeoman (2) are preparing to hoist Nelson's final signal of the day – 'engage the enemy more closely'. Meanwhile Captain Berry of the *Vanguard* (3) and the flag lieutenant (4) are keeping Nelson company during these crucial minutes, before the pair move to their final battle positions on the quarterdeck, leaving the poop deck to the marine sharpshooters and the signallers.

obscured from the other by a combination of darkness and fog. This was one of the great 'what if' moments in history. If Nelson had come upon the French in daylight, he would undoubtedly have defeated Brueys, and captured, sunk or scattered the convoy of transports. Therefore the career of General Bonaparte might have ended before it had fully begun.

Nelson was risking a lot by continuing his pursuit into the Eastern Mediterranean. The invasion force might be heading north into the Adriatic, or might be doubling back to invade Sicily. He was relying on little more than instinct. The faster-sailing British ships actually overtook the French, and on 28 June Nelson's fleet reached Alexandria, the Egyptian port he surmised the French were heading for. Finding it empty was a bitter blow, making it look all the more likely that Brueys had doubled back, and had sailed north or west. Nelson wasted no time in heading back out to sea, heading north towards the Turkish coast, before swinging westwards again towards Crete and Greece.

Two days after Nelson sailed from Alexandria the French appeared. Again, had Nelson waited to take on water or supplies history might have taken a different course. As it was the French were able to disembark their army in peace. On 7 July, Brueys left the transports off Alexandria and took his fleet 15 miles along the coast to Aboukir Bay, where it was less exposed to attack. Shoals, islands and gun batteries protected his anchorage, and by mooring in line astern Brueys hoped to cover the remaining seaward approach with the guns of his fleet.

On 19 July Nelson reached Sicily, but there was no sign of the French. It was now clear that Alexandria had been the destination, and that somehow the two fleets had missed each other. Once more, Nelson set off in pursuit. The weeks of searching hadn't been completely wasted though. Nelson regularly summoned his captains on board the flagship, two or three at a time, and discussed tactics over dinner. Consequently, by the time the British fleet reached Alexandria again on 1 August and saw the French transports there, all of his captains knew exactly what was expected of them.

Nelson's doctrine revolved round the complete destruction of the enemy. To achieve this he planned to bring superior force against the vital portion of the enemy fleet. In effect, he would use the same blitzkrieg tactics the Germans used almost a century and a half later, only using sailing ships of war.

As there was no sign of the enemy battle fleet Nelson sent ships ahead, who soon came upon the French in Aboukir Bay. Nelson decided to attack immediately. That afternoon, Vice-Amiral Brueys had sent many

Horatio Nelson, having caught the French fleet – depicted here as a congregation of crocodiles – proceeds to club them to death. In this cartoon version of the battle of the Nile, a crocodile representing *L'Orient* explodes behind the naval hero.

The battle of the Nile, 1 August 1798

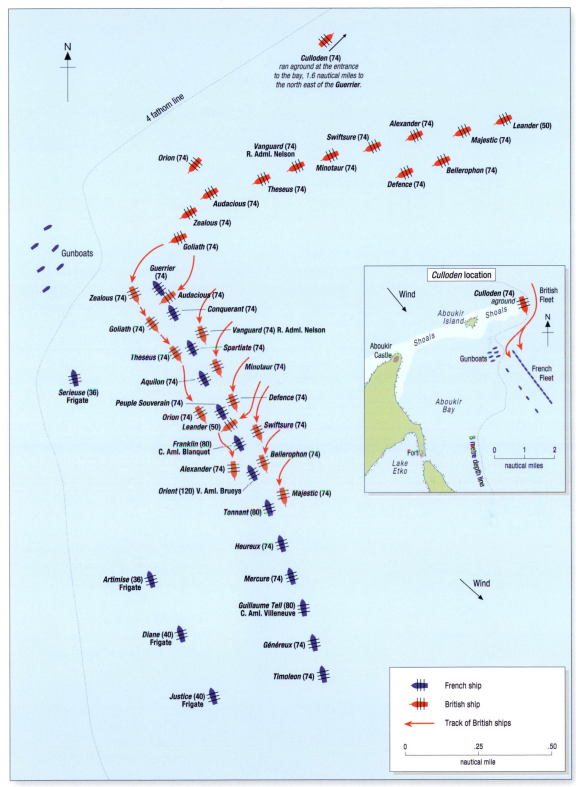

of his men ashore to collect fresh water and supplies. When the British appeared these men were still on the shore, and therefore took no part in the battle that followed. The French ships-of-the-line were anchored in a long line, facing towards Aboukir Island to the north-west. The French line lay close to the 4-fathom mark – the depth of keel of a typical fully laden ship-of-the-line. Anchored in this shallow water was a small flotilla of gunboats, while four French frigates lay a few cables to landward of the fleet.

The British approached in line astern from the east, and at 6.15pm – dusk on 1 August – the French gunners on Aboukir Castle opened fire. At 6.30pm Nelson rounded the shoals to the north of Aboukir Island. Sunset was at 6.44pm, and when he spotted the British Brueys expected them to lie off until morning, giving him plenty of time to prepare for the battle ahead. He hadn't reckoned with Nelson, who immediately hoisted the signal 'Prepare for Battle'. To be more accurate, his signal also added '… and for anchoring with springs'. This was highly unusual. His intention was for his fleet to pass through the narrow gaps between the French ships, come alongside them and then drop anchor so they could pound the enemy into submission. By passing springs through the stern gunports, additional anchors could be laid out astern. The ships could then be moved around slightly, making sure they would always be ranged against their target.

Culloden ran aground on the shoals, but the rest of the fleet passed her to seaward, and safely entered the bay. They headed south, at which point Nelson ran up two signals in quick succession. These told his captains to concentrate on the front and centre of the French line, to abandon any formal line and to approach and attack the enemy at their discretion. In other words he planned to overwhelm the front half of the French fleet, which lay to windward of the rest. His ships could then work their way down the line. He was also leaving the tactical decisions to his captains – the men he trusted to do his bidding. His final signal remained flying throughout the course of the battle. It read 'Engage the enemy more closely'.

Of Nelson's 14 ships-of-the-line, the *Culloden* had run aground. The remaining British ships were – in order – the *Goliath, Zealous, Audacious, Orion, Theseus,* the flagship *Vanguard, Minotaur, Swiftsure, Defence, Alexander, Bellerophon, Majestic* and finally the 50-gun *Leander*. Captain Foley of the *Goliath* was well aware that Nelson wanted to concentrate his fleet against a portion of the enemy force. Consequently he passed the leading French ship – the *Guerrier* (74), raking her as he did so. Gambling that there was sufficient water to starboard, he turned and passed down the port side of the French line. The French were completely unprepared for this,

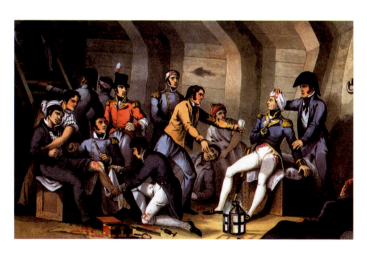

Nelson was wounded in the forehead during the battle of the Nile. The ship's surgeon Michael Jefferson tended and dressed the wound. After a brief opiate-induced respite Nelson then returned on deck to watch the conclusion of the battle.

having doubled up their gun crews on the starboard side. The *Goliath* blasted the next French ship *Conquerant* (74) without her firing back, and Foley dropped anchor between her and the *Spartiate* (74), the third ship in the French line. The next four British ships did the same, rounding the enemy line to engage it from the landward side. All of them anchored and opened fire on the leading three French ships, apart from Captain Saumarez of the *Orion*, who passed the *Aquilon* (74) astern of the *Spartiate*, to engage the fifth French ship, the *Peuple Souverain* (74).

The rest of the British fleet bore down on the starboard side of the French line. Nelson in the *Vanguard* engaged the *Spartiate*, while the *Minotaur* and *Defence* ranged alongside the *Aquilon* and *Peuple Souverain*. The little *Leander* passed between this fifth French ship and the one astern of her, the *Franklin* (80), before anchoring so she could rake both ships without the enemy firing back. Finally the *Swiftsure*, *Bellerophon* and *Alexander* clustered themselves around Bruey's flagship, the first rate *L'Orient* (120). Finally the *Majestic* fired into the *Heureux* (74) as she passed her, two ships astern of the French flagship, but dropped her anchor next to the *Mercure* (74), the tenth ship in the French line.

These tactics proved devastating. The French ships were already short of men, as up to a quarter of their crews were still ashore. This made it difficult to fire their guns to both sides, and not only could the British crews fire faster, in most cases they were pouring fire into both sides of the French ships. Due to the north-westerly wind the remainder of the French ships were unable to come to the rescue of their compatriots. It was also extremely hazardous to try to raise anchor and escape to windward in the pitch dark. What followed was therefore a textbook demonstration of Nelson's doctrine involving the concentration of superior force.

It was now dark, but the flashes of gunfire lit up the bay as one by one the French ships were pounded into submission. The frigate *Serieuse* had opened fire on the *Orion*, and Saumarez returned fire so effectively the frigate was holed and sunk, while his port gun crews concentrated on the *Peuple Souverain*. The first of the French ships to strike her colours was the *Guerrier*, which by 8pm was a dismasted hulk. Nelson in the *Vanguard* was engaging the *Spartiate*, but was also fired on from *Aquilon* until the *Minotaur* and *Theseus* ranged up on both sides of her. At around 8pm Nelson was wounded by a piece of flying metal, and was taken below, his face covered in blood. As he was carried away he exclaimed to Captain Berry; 'I am killed!' In fact, it was only a superficial wound, which caused a flap of skin to temporarily

The defining moment of the battle of the Nile came at around 9.30pm, when the French flagship *L'Orient* exploded. The moment was captured in this dramatic but wholly inaccurate engraving. For several minutes afterwards the onlookers were too stunned to continue fighting.

cover his good eye. Once the blood was cleaned away and the wound dressed Nelson was encouraged to rest. However, when a sailor brought news that the French flagship was burning he returned to the quarterdeck.

By that time the *Spartiate* had surrendered, as had most of the other leading French ships, and the battle was centred around *L'Orient*. When the battle began the *Swiftsure* and *Bellerophon* moved up to engage her on her starboard side, while the *Alexander* passed *L'Orient* to engage her to port. Brueys concentrated his fire on the *Bellerophon*, which was soon dismasted. When her anchor cable parted she drifted off into the darkness and out of the fight. Meanwhile the dismasted *Peuple Souverain* had cut her cable and drifted stern-first past the *Franklin*. That was when the *Leander* moved into the gap she left, and took up a raking position in front of the *Franklin's* bow.

Vice-Amiral Brueys had been lightly wounded early in the battle, but he remained at his post until a roundshot cut off his legs. The dying admiral still refused to be taken below, but had the surgeon apply a tourniquet around both stumps. Minutes later he was decapitated by another roundshot. By then it was 9pm, and the flagship was ablaze. On board the *Swiftsure* the heat melted the pitch in her deck, and she pulled back slightly, out of the way. *L'Orient* continued to fire until 9.37pm, when the flames reached her magazine. The majestic French flagship was literally ripped apart, the explosion throwing debris hundreds of feet into the air. Over 1,000 men went down with their ship.

By that time the battle was reaching its final stages. The British ships ranged down the French line, and shortly after 11pm the *Franklin* surrendered, followed minutes later by the *Tonnant* (80) which was anchored astern of the flagship, and had been damaged in the explosion. Further astern the *Heureux* and *Mercure* cut their cables and ran themselves aground. While this saved the crews, the two ships were captured by the British. That left the last three ships in the French line, the *Guillaume Tell*, *Généreux* and *Timoleon*, all 74s. The first two managed to cut their cables and escape into the night, the *Guillaume Tell* still flying the flag of Contre-Amiral (Rear-Admiral)

The battle of the Nile was fought at night, the carnage lit by the burning French flagship *L'Orient*. In this scene boat crews from both fleets are shown rescuing survivors from the water, many of them wounded or burnt.

Villeneuve, who would face Nelson at Trafalgar seven years later. Two frigates also made it to safety, but the *Timoleon* wasn't so fortunate, losing her masts when she ran aground where she was forced to surrender.

The engagement known as the battle of the Nile was a stunning victory. Virtually an entire French fleet had been destroyed, and Nelson's doctrine had been proved in battle. If he had done nothing else in his career Nelson would have been remembered as a great admiral for his achievement that day – 1 August 1798. Instead, there would be yet more stunning victories to come.

Nelson in Naples, 1798–1800

Since the spring of 1795 Nelson's star had been in the ascendant. Then, for over a year, he seemed to abandon everything in his pursuit of a married woman. It all began on 22 September 1798 when Nelson's victorious fleet put into Naples, which was then an anti-French bastion. The British ambassador and his wife, Sir William and Lady Hamilton, were rowed out to the *Vanguard*, accompanied by King Ferdinand of the Two Sicilies and his senior naval commander, Commodore Caracciolo. Ferdinand was a notoriously weak king, and the effective ruler of Naples was his wife Queen Maria Carolina, a sister of Marie Antoinette. Nelson later wrote to his wife, describing Emma Hamilton as 'one of the very best women in the world'. His infatuation had already begun.

Nelson became embroiled in the murky world of Neapolitan politics. First, he offered to transport Neapolitan troops to Leghorn – part of a Neapolitan drive up the Italian peninsula. This came to naught after the French soundly routed King Ferdinand's army at Castellana, just beyond Rome. Meanwhile Nelson was supposed to be blockading the French on Malta, but apart from the capture of the garrison on Gozo little was achieved there. Instead, in late December Nelson and his ships transported the Neapolitan royal family and the Hamiltons to Palermo in Sicily.

For the next six months Nelson remained in Palermo, living ashore with the Hamiltons while his subordinates blockaded Naples, which was now in French hands, and Malta. During the summer of 1799 a populist uprising drove the French from Naples, while Nelson was drawn away in pursuit of Vice-Admiral Bruix, whose French fleet had put to sea from Toulon. Forewarned by his frigates, Bruix ran back into port before Nelson could catch him. With the French dealt with, Nelson sailed to Naples, to help re-establish royal authority there. One of the republican rebels who sided with the French the previous year was Commodore Caracciolo. He was duly tried on board Nelson's new flagship *Foudrayant*, and hanged from the yardarm of a Neapolitan frigate.

Nelson played little part in the siege of Malta (1798–1800), apart from thwarting an attempt to relieve the island in February 1800. The French garrison finally surrendered the following September. In this scene of the capitulation, the garrison commander General Vaubois greets Captain Martin.

The Neapolitan naval commander Commodore Francesco Caracciolo (1752–99) defected to the French, but was captured and hanged from the yardarm of his own flagship. In this melodramatic scene Nelson, the Hamiltons and King Ferdinand watch his body float past Nelson's flagship.

Once again, Nelson was deeply mired in Neapolitan politics. He was also neglecting his duty.

In July, Lord Keith, who now commanded the Mediterranean Fleet ordered Nelson to Port Mahon in Minorca, where a naval base had been established. Nelson ignored this order and a second demand from Lord Keith, claiming the situation in Naples warranted he remain there. When a third demand arrived, Nelson sent four ships and remained in Naples with the bulk of his fleet. This was an act of gross insubordination, compounded by Nelson's decision to spend the winter at Palermo living ashore with the Hamiltons. Sir William was 67, and his wife Emma – a former maid, dancer and mistress – was just 23. The ambassador seemed more interested in Italian antiquities than in his young wife, and he may even have encouraged the friendship of Emma with the admiral. In any event, by Christmas, Emma had become Nelson's mistress.

His dalliance in Palermo was unfortunate – the blockade and siege of Malta wasn't prosecuted with any vigour and Napoleon Bonaparte managed to slip through the Mediterranean from Egypt to reach France in October 1799. In January 1800 Lord Keith arrived in person to spur Nelson into action. The two admirals combined forces to reinforce the besiegers of Malta, and as a bonus Nelson intercepted and captured the *Généreux*, one of the two French ships-of-the-line to escape from Aboukir Bay. The other, the *Guillaume Tell*, was blockaded in Malta. When Nelson sailed to Leghorn with Queen Maria on board, Lord Keith lost his patience and sailed there too to

Nelson actively supported Naples between 1798 and 1800, as he saw the kingdom as a useful counter to French expansionist plans in Italy. Here his ships lie at anchor in the Bay of Naples, the vista dominated by Mount Vesuvius.

dress down his subordinate. On 24 June he declared that 'Lady Hamilton has had control of the fleet for long enough', and Nelson was ordered back to Britain. He struck his flag on 13 July, but rather than return by sea he chose to accompany the Hamiltons on their own journey home, travelling through Austria and Germany.

This whole episode and his blatant love affair with a married woman did Nelson no favours. Old friends and colleagues cut their ties with him, and even St Vincent disapproved of his dalliance. Nelson spent 3½ months on his rambling tour of Europe, and finally reached Yarmouth in November 1800. He had fallen so far from favour in the Admiralty that he might well have been sidelined for the remainder of the war. As it was, his services were soon required again.

The battle of Copenhagen, 1801

In December 1800 Russia, Denmark and Sweden signed an armed neutrality pact, whereby they declared their neutrality in the war between Britain and France, but maintained the right to defend themselves, and the right of their ships to trade where they pleased. Clearly this would make a mockery of the Continental blockade imposed on France by the British. The brainchild of the pro-French Tsar Paul I, the pact was effectively an alliance with France, and it raised the spectre of these three Baltic nations adding their naval strength to that of France. The British Government saw this neutrality pact as a major threat and decided to react accordingly.

Consequently Admiral Sir Hyde Parker was ordered to lead a fleet into the Baltic in an attempt to coerce the three powers to abandon their pact. In January 1801, Nelson hoisted his flag in his old Spanish prize the *San Josef* (previously *San José*), now part of the Channel Fleet. However, with this new crisis looming Nelson was ordered to join the fleet gathering in Yarmouth for service in the Baltic. There he would serve as Parker's second-in-command, flying his flag in the *St George* (98). Parker was an undistinguished commander, and seemed more interested in his new young wife than his duty. Nelson, having been recently accused of a similar dereliction, was eager to make amends. In different circumstances Nelson might have led the expedition, but the Emma Hamilton scandal made that impossible.

The fleet sailed on 12 May, and two weeks later it reached the Kattegat, and lay off the northern entrance of The Sound, the narrow well-defended channel between Sweden and the Danish island of Sælland. Parker was unsure what to do next. The Russian fleet was icebound at Reval on the Gulf of Finland, while the smaller Swedish

Before the battle of Copenhagen Nelson dined with his captains, when he told them his plan, and what was expected of them. This stylized view of the breakfast shows the officers toasting a leading wind, and success later that day.

In this copy of a well-known painting of the battle of Copenhagen by Nicolas Pocock, Nelson's ships are shown engaging the Danish defensive line, with the city behind them, while in the foreground bomb vessels fire on the Trekroner Fort.

fleet was wintering in its fortified base at Karlskrona in southern Sweden. That left the Danish Fleet, which was based in Copenhagen at the far end of the Sound. After more indecisiveness Parker elected to lead his fleet through The Sound, past the Danish fortress of Elsinore, the setting for Shakespeare's *Hamlet*. By keeping to the Swedish side the British worked their way past this fortification, and, by the start of April Parker's fleet lay within sight of Copenhagen. Attempts to reach a diplomatic solution had failed, and when the Danes interned British merchant ships, Parker was left with no option but to attack.

The Danish Fleet lay in Copenhagen itself, close to the Nyholm dockyard. The only approach to the city was along the narrow Kronlobet Channel, which was guarded by batteries on the seaward side of the city, and by the Trekroner Fort, a sea fort built where the channel entered the wider Konigs-tief (King's Deep). Sandbanks prevented ships in this waterway from approaching close to the Danish shore, and a line of four floating batteries and 14 moored hulks lining the western edge of the Konigs-tief further strengthened the defences. Yet more hulks lined the Kronlobet, creating a formidable line of defences, designed to keep any attacker out of range of the dockyard, the main anchorage and the city.

It was clear that a frontal attack on the port would be difficult and costly. While Parker was deterred, Nelson spotted the weakness in the Danish defence. If an attack could be launched against the southern end of the defensive line in the Konigs-tief, then the British could then work their way up the line of hulks and ships, overwhelming the defenders with massed firepower as they went. With the line gone, the British could then bring up their mortar boats to bombard the ships in the harbour. Parker agreed, and Nelson was ordered to put the plan into operation.

Nelson was given command of the 12 lightest ships-of-the-line in the fleet, and a squadron of frigates and smaller vessels. He transferred his flag to the *Elephant* (74), and ordered soundings to be taken and buoys laid to mark the Holland Deep – the channel his ships would use to reach the southern end of the Konigs-tief. This channel lay at the far side of the Middle Ground Shoal, a sandbank that prevented Nelson from making a direct assault against the Konigs-tief. His fleet would need to pass through this channel in order to reach their starting positions. During the evening of 1 April Nelson's ships passed through the 4-mile-long Holland Deep, to reach their night-time anchorage off the southern tip of the Middle Ground Shoal. That evening Nelson issued his final orders, and waited for dawn and a suitable wind. He was in good spirits and eager for battle. Still, this was

The battle of Copenhagen, 2 April 1801

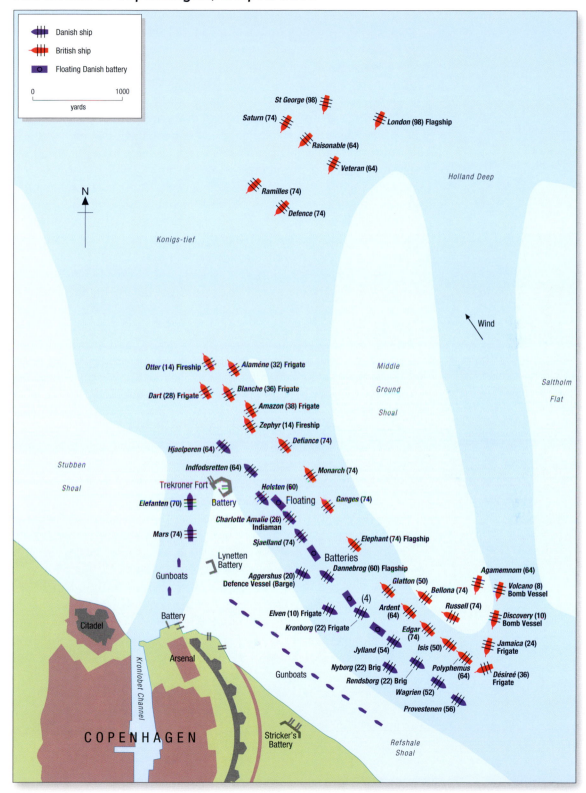

Danish ship
British ship
Floating Danish battery

0   1000
yards

St George (98)
Saturn (74)
London (98) Flagship
Raisonable (64)
Veteran (64)
Ramilles (74)
Defence (74)

Holland Deep

N

Konigs-tief

Wind

Saltholm
Flat

Otter (14) Fireship
Alaméne (32) Frigate
Blanche (36) Frigate
Dart (28) Frigate
Amazon (38) Frigate
Zephyr (14) Fireship
Defiance (74)

Middle
Ground
Shoal

Hjaelperen (64)
Indfodsretten (64)
Monarch (74)

Stubben
Shoal

Trekroner Fort
Holsten (60)
Floating
Ganges (74)
Elefanten (70)
Battery
Charlotte Amalie (26)
Indiaman
Mars (74)
Sjaelland (74)
Elephant (74) Flagship
Lynetten
Battery
Batteries
Gunboats
Dannebrog (60) Flagship
Aggershus (20)
Agamemnom (64)
Defence Vessel (Barge)
Glatton (50)
Bellona (74)
Volcano (8)
Bomb Vessel
(4)
Elven (10) Frigate
Ardent
(64)
Russell (74)
Battery
Kronborg (22) Frigate
Edgar
(74)
Discovery (10)
Bomb Vessel
Citadel
Jylland (54)
Isis (50)
Jamaica (24)
Frigate
Arsenal
Nyborg (22) Brig
Polyphemus
(64)
Désireé (36)
Frigate
Gunboats
Rendsborg (22) Brig
Wagrien (52)
Provestenen (56)

COPENHAGEN

Stricker's
Battery

Refshale
Shoal

a harrowing time, as there was a danger that the Danes would bring up mortars to shell the anchorage, or reinforce the hulks in their defensive line.

As dawn broke on the morning of 2 April Nelson must have been relieved that no such bombardment had taken place, and that the brisk wind was from the south-south-east – the perfect direction for the attack. He called his captains to the *Elephant* for breakfast – a typical Nelson gesture as it gave him the chance to issue his orders in person, and to make sure that all his captains knew exactly what he expected of them. It was just what he had done before the battle of the Nile – a gathering that allowed him as much to enthuse his commanders with his own aggressive spirit as to make sure they all knew what to do once the shooting started.

Nelson suspected that the Danes had anchored their hulks and floating batteries along the western edge of the channel, leaving him no room to pass ships between them and the shore, as he had done at the Nile. Instead, he would have to overwhelm them with firepower from the seaward side. He divided his ships into three groups. Five ships-of-the-line – *Edgar* (74), *Ardent* (64), *Glatton* (56), *Isis* (50) and *Agamemnon* (64) would anchor in front of the lower half of the line, and begin a gun duel with their Danish opponents. A second more powerful group – *Bellona*, *Russell*, *Elephant*, *Ganges*, *Monarch* and *Defiance* (all 74s) would fire on the same targets as they sailed past, but their task was to engage the northern portion of the line.

Once the first group had overwhelmed their opponents they would move to support them. Finally Captain Riou's frigate squadron would divert the fire of the Trekroner Fort, and act as a link between Nelson and Parker. Once the line was overwhelmed, Parker would bring the rest of the fleet forward to support Riou. The plan was bold, ambitious and relied on the superiority of British gunnery to win the day. Nelson was also counting on his pilots to guide the fleet towards their targets. Their initial hesitation was overcome by the master of the *Bellona*, who offered to lead the fleet into the Konigs-tief. In the end *Bellona*, *Russell* and *Agamemnon* ran aground, but at least the first two were in range of the enemy and able to play their part in the coming battle. The rest of the fleet made it through the tricky passage, and by 10am the two lines of ships had began unleashing crippling broadsides at each other, fired at a range of just under 400 yards (365m).

The second group of British ships fired into the Danish hulks as they majestically sailed past them, although with two of their number aground their close-range firepower was somewhat reduced. The *Elephant* was in the thick of the fighting, and was cheered by the men of the *Bellona* as she sailed past them, heading for the northern part of the Danish line. Throughout the battle Nelson again flew signal 16 – 'Engage the enemy more closely'. That is exactly what his captains did.

The Danish fire was extremely heavy – greater than Nelson had anticipated – but their defensive line was outgunned by the British ships, whose crews affirmed Nelson's faith in their abilities. They poured a torrent of close-range fire into the hulks and floating batteries, shattering their targets, disabling their guns and rendering them vulnerable to capture.

The battle of Copenhagen, seen from the Danish perspective. A pall of smoke hangs over Nelson's ships as they engage the northern portion of the Danish line. The foreground is dominated by the Danish Royal dockyard and arsenal. Engraving by Johan Clemens.

Nelson's force was accompanied by soldiers of the 49th Foot, under orders to storm the enemy vessels if the opportunity presented itself. In the end there was little need. This battle would be won by firepower, and the roundshot, barshot and grapeshot continued to fly.

Shortly after 11am the smallest of the Danish vessels began to pull out of the line, cutting their mooring cables in an effort to reach the comparative safety of the shallows behind the Trekroner Fort. First to go was the *Rendsborg* (22), followed by the *Nyborg* (22), which sank as she withdrew. Commodore Fischer's flagship *Dannebrog* (60) was set ablaze, forcing the Danish commander to transfer his flag to the *Holsten* (60) further up the line to the north. The *Dannebrog* was abandoned, and burned to the waterline. Two Danish floating batteries sank at their moorings, and by 1pm the *Wagrien* (52) and *Jylland* (70) had struck their colours.

However, the fighting was far from one-sided. *Monarch*, *Ganges* and *Defiance* were all badly damaged and had to haul out of the line, running aground on the eastern side of the channel, within range of the guns of Trekroner Fort. Rear-Admiral Graves in the *Defiance* later described the battle as 'the hottest action that has happened this war'. On board the *Elephant*, Nelson was watching the course of the battle, accompanied by the flagship's commander, Captain Foley, and Lieutenant-Colonel Stewart of the 49th Foot. Stewart claimed Nelson had turned to him when the battle was at its height and said that it was warm work, but 'I should not be anywhere else for thousands'. He also observed that 'these fellows hold us a better jig than expected', but he never doubted his fleet would prevail.

It was then that a signal broke out on Parker's flagship the *London*. It was signal 39 – 'Discontinue the engagement'. The Admiral was almost 4 miles away to the north-east. To him it must have looked like the Danish line was holding – he was unable to see the carnage being inflicted on Commodore Fischer's ships. Nelson ordered the signal to be acknowledged, but kept flying signal 16 from his own masthead. According to Stewart, Nelson turned to Foley, and exclaimed 'You know Foley, I have only one eye. I have a right to be blind sometimes.' He put his telescope to his bad eye, and added 'I really do not see the signal'. Nelson knew that victory lay within his grasp, and once again he was prepared to disobey orders to win the day.

The signal wasn't repeated, nor did Nelson's leading subordinate, Rear-Admiral Graves in the *Defiance*, take it up. Further to the north, Captain Riou had little option but to obey the signal. After all, Parker was less than 2 miles away. He gave the order for his frigate squadron to disengage, exclaiming as he did so 'What will Nelson think of us?' As his 36-gun flagship *Amazon* turned away she presented her stern to Trekroner Fort, who raked the frigate, and Riou

True perspective is ignored in this depiction of the battle of Copenhagen by John Bang. Instead the action is stylized, and while Nelson engages the Danish line, bomb vessels fire on the city defences, while Hyde Parker's ships lie in reserve.

was cut in two by a roundshot as it sliced through his ship. It showed just how dangerous a full-scale disengagement would have been. The Danes could have snatched a surprise victory from the jaws of imminent defeat. Fortunately for the British cause, the rest of the engaged ships followed Nelson's lead, and the battle continued.

The tide of battle had already turned. The Danes were abandoning the batteries and hulks in the central and southern portions of their line. The firing began to slacken, and in the south it died out altogether. This also allowed the British ships anchored in the south to work their way northwards to engage the northern part of the Danish line. This meant that the British were able to concentrate their fire on the Danes who were still making a fight of it. By 2pm these last Danish commanders began to bow to the inevitable and surrender. *Charlotte Amalie* (26), the battery *Sohesten* and the *Holsten* all struck, while Fischer withdrew to the Trekroner Fort.

It was at that point that Nelson showed that his diplomatic skills were just as well honed as his tactical ones. At 2pm he penned a letter suggesting an armistice. By that stage the Trekroner Fort was still in action, and the rest of the Danish line had been silenced, but not captured. Nelson's threat was that he would burn the remaining batteries and hulks if the Danes refused to agree. That meant the grisly death of many hundreds of wounded Danish sailors. The alternative meant that the wounded would be put ashore, while Nelson secured his prizes. The Danes had little option but to agree, and, while negotiations would continue, the battle officially came to an end.

Nelson took possession of 12 of the Danish ships, but he burned all of them except the *Holsten*, which he considered worthy of being repaired and commissioned into the Royal Navy. The following morning Nelson brought up his bomb vessels, but they held their fire while the negotiations got under way in earnest. Nelson went ashore to meet the Danish Crown Prince, and demanded that the country withdraw from its armed neutrality pact. The Danes were hesitant as they feared Russian reprisals, but faced with the imminent bombardment of their capital there was little room for negotiation. Then came the news that pro-French Tsar Paul had died in a palace coup, and the new tsar, Alexander I, was unlikely to honour his father's pact. A deal was arranged. Denmark would abandon the pact and the British would spare the fleet and the city.

The victory made Nelson a national hero – again. His reputation had been badly tarnished by his affair with Lady Hamilton, but that was now forgotten as Nelson was lauded as a conquering hero. Parker's role in the campaign was all but forgotten – in fact he was recalled to Britain shortly after the battle, leaving Nelson to bring the campaign to a close. As the Russians and Swedes refused to give battle there was little more he could do, and by 1 July Nelson was back in Britain, while Vice-Admiral Pole replaced him as commander of the Baltic Fleet. Nelson became a Viscount, but further honours were denied him, as, with peace with Denmark assured, the Government was eager to draw a diplomatic line under the whole business.

From Boulogne to Toulon

On his return Nelson cut all ties with his wife Fanny and instead bought Merton Place, a house near Wimbledon that he shared with Emma Hamilton and her ageing husband. That summer the French were preparing an invasion fleet, and their army was encamped around the Channel ports. Therefore St Vincent, now the First Lord of the Admiralty, ordered Nelson to take command of the British counter-invasion fleet gathered in the Downs, with responsibility for defending the coast from Orfordness in Suffolk round to Beachy Head in East Sussex. This included the most likely invasion beaches near Dover, at the narrowest point in the Channel.

Nelson spent several months at sea, as well as touring the shore defences of his command. He also restructured the organization of the fleet, making it able to respond quickly to any French invasion attempt. Nelson was confident he could destroy the French before they reached the British coast, but both he and St Vincent were also keen to take the war to the enemy. He reconnoitred the French Channel ports, and in August he launched an unsuccessful raid on Boulogne. Just like at Tenerife, the local current thwarted Nelson's attempt to send boats in to cut out the invasion barges, and as casualties mounted Nelson called off the assault.

In October the Peace of Amiens was signed between Britain and France, and Nelson, suffering from neuralgia and gum disease, was finally able to haul down his flag. He joined the Hamiltons at Merton, and the *ménage à trois* continued, although neither Sir William nor Viscount Nelson shared Emma's love of dinner parties or extravagant receptions. Both men were in poor health, although Nelson did attend the House

The waiting room at the Admiralty, where officers, civilian contractors, prize agents and aspiring midshipmen wait their turn to be seen. It was in a room such as this that Nelson met the future Duke of Wellington in September 1805.

39

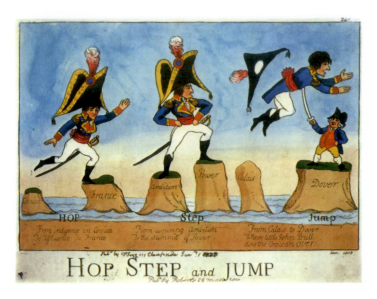

The image contains the labels: France, Ambition, Power, Calais, Dover, HOP, Step, Jump, and the title "HOP STEP and JUMP". Additional text reads: "From indigence in Corsica / To Affluence in France", "From aspiring ambition / To the summit of Power", "From Calais to Dover / where little John Bull / does the Corsican OVER".

The threat of French invasion was very real indeed – between 1803 and 1805 only the vigilance of the Royal Navy prevented General Bonaparte's troops from attempting the crossing. In this cartoon of 1803, 'John Bull' is ready and waiting for 'The Corsican'.

of Lords where he spoke in favour of the current government. The trio also toured Sir William's holdings in England and Wales, where Nelson was universally celebrated as the great national hero he had become. Still, Sir William's health declined steadily, and in April 1803 he died, worn out, it was unkindly rumoured, by the behaviour of his unfaithful wife.

In theory this might have allowed Nelson and Emma Hamilton to put their relationship on a more honourable footing. Instead, war intervened. The Peace of Amiens was never more than a temporary cessation of hostilities, a useful historical comma used to divide the French Revolutionary Wars from the campaigns of Napoleon. On 16 May Britain declared war on France, and ten days before Nelson was appointed as the new commander of the Mediterranean Fleet. He left Merton and travelled down to Portsmouth, hoisting his flag in his new flagship HMS *Victory* on 18 May – the day the declaration of war was formally acknowledged by the French. Two days later he was at sea, bound for Malta. He transferred to the frigate *Amphion* to make a faster passage and reached Malta four weeks after his departure from Portsmouth. Once again he was charged with thwarting French interests in the region, safeguarding Naples and Sicily, and denying the French access to the trading ports of the Mediterranean. It was a demanding assignment, but Nelson was more than equal to the challenge.

First though, was the tedious, unremitting business of blockading the French fleet at Toulon. Nelson began the blockade with eight worn-out ships-of-the-line, and for two years they remained on station, with only the occasional chance for a ship to slip away to Gibraltar for refit and repair. Apart from *Victory*, only three other ships-of-the-line arrived as reinforcements, so Nelson had to keep his fleet concentrated off the enemy port, where the enemy enjoyed parity of numbers. It was a testimony to Nelson's abilities that this force could spend two years at sea without collectively putting into a friendly port, and then manage to chase the enemy to the West Indies and back, before fighting a major battle.

The problem was, the Royal Navy was thinly stretched, particularly as it was apparent that Spain, although still neutral, was openly siding with France. In December 1804 the Spanish declared war on Britain, and this forced the British to divert ships to blockade the ports of Cadiz, Vigo and Ferrol. The invasion of Britain remained a significant threat, but as both St Vincent and Nelson knew, the French lacked the strength to fight their way across the English Channel. As St Vincent put it when addressing

Parliament, 'I don't say that the French can't come – only they can't come by sea.' The risk, though, was that the French Mediterranean and Channel fleets might join forces with the Spanish. Then St Vincent would be hard pressed to prevent an invasion.

Nelson knew this and wanted to reduce the risk by defeating the French before they could make such an attempt. As he put it in August 1804: 'The port of Toulon has never been blockaded by me. Quite the reverse – every opportunity has been offered to the enemy to put to sea, for it is there that we hope to realise the hopes and expectations of our country.' However, for the moment the French remained resolutely in port, although it was clear that in all the major French and Spanish ports, ships were being readied for sea. The decisive naval campaign of the war was about to begin.

Nelson described Merton Place in Surrey as a beloved place, home to his mistress Emma and their daughter Horatia. Nelson bought the property in September 1801, and he spent his last days in Britain there during August and September 1805.

The pursuit

The French finally made their move on 18 January, under cover of a winter storm. Nelson's fleet was riding the gale out off the north-eastern corner of Sardinia when his frigates raced in with the news that the French were out. Vice-Amiral Villeneuve's fleet could be making for Cadiz, Malta or Egypt, and Nelson moved to the southern side of Sardinia, hoping to intercept the enemy if they headed east. The long-awaited battle never materialized, as the French were scattered and damaged by the storm, and Villeneuve decided to slip back into Toulon after just three days at sea. Still, it was clear that something was afoot and that the French were going to try again.

In fact, Villeneuve's attempted breakout was only part of a much larger plan. He was expected to rendezvous with the Spanish, then sail with them to the West Indies. There the Channel Fleet would join them, once it broke the blockade of Brest. Then the joint armada would descend on the English Channel. Villeneuve sailed again on 30 March, with 11 ships-of-the-line. He headed south to avoid Nelson and his 12 ships-of-the-line, which were reportedly cruising off Barcelona. In fact Nelson was to the south, off Sardinia, lying in wait. On 1 April, Villeneuve broke off to the west after learning from a merchantman that Nelson lay ahead of him. By 6 April he was off Cartagena, but the six Spanish ships-of-the-line there weren't ready to join him. Villeneuve pressed on, passing through the Straits of Gibraltar to rendezvous with the main Spanish fleet off Cadiz on 8 April. That brought the Allied strength up to 18 ships-of-the-line. Accompanied by his Spanish counterpart, Teniente-General Gravina, Villeneuve then set a course for the West Indies.

Nelson gave chase, but he had no idea where Villeneuve was heading. The small British force of six ships-of-the-line off Cadiz had withdrawn

to Lagos Bay south of Lisbon, and Nelson joined them there on 9 May. That was when he learned that Villeneuve was probably sailing west across the Atlantic. The following day he set off in pursuit – a gamble based on an educated guess. On 4 June Nelson reached Barbados, where he discovered his hunch was correct. Villeneuve had reached Martinique on 14 May, but apart from capturing the British garrison on Diamond Rock and harassing local shipping, he had done little to damage British interests in the West Indies. Instead, disease was sweeping through the French fleet, and Villeneuve landed over 1,000 invalids. On hearing that Nelson was in pursuit he decided he couldn't linger and wait for the Brest fleet. After collecting two more third rates in the West Indies, Villeneuve headed back out into the Atlantic, bound for northern Spain.

Nelson's last flagship was HMS *Victory*, a 100-gun first rate launched in 1765. Before Nelson hoisted his flag in her in May 1803 she had already seen action in three major sea battles, as the flagship of Admirals Keppel, Kempenfelt and Jervis.

Nelson had only limited information at his disposal, not all of which was accurate. Nevertheless he divined Villeneuve's intentions, and took the great gamble to follow him into the Atlantic. If Nelson were wrong the sugar islands of the West Indies, Britain's richest colonies, would be exposed to attack. However, Nelson was thinking offensively. His objective was nothing short of the destruction of the Franco-Spanish fleet. Therefore, leaving one ship in the West Indies, he set a course to the east with his remaining 11 ships-of-the-line.

Even if Villeneuve was recrossing the Atlantic, Nelson didn't know if his destination was Brest, Vigo or Cadiz. He relied on the Channel Fleet to prevent Villeneuve from reaching Brest, so he steered towards Gibraltar in the hope of bringing about a decisive battle off Cadiz, regardless of the odds. Before he left the West Indies Nelson sent the brig *Curieux* to Britain with dispatches, and it sighted the French fleet in the mid-Atlantic as it sped past it towards Plymouth. The new First Lord of the Admiralty, Lord Barham, immediately issued the orders needed to bring Villeneuve to bay. The blockading squadrons off Ferrol and Rochefort would combine, forming a fleet of 15 ships-of-the-line under Vice-Admiral Calder, which was to be stationed off Cape Finisterre, the north-west tip of Spain.

Villeneuve's fleet was sighted on 22 July, but Calder was hesitant and failed to bring about a decisive battle. Instead Villeneuve slipped past him into the Spanish ports of Ferrol and Vigo. Calder left a small squadron of observation, and rejoined Admiral Cornwallis' Channel Fleet off Brest. Meanwhile Nelson had reached Gibraltar two days before Calder's action, and immediately sailed north again. He joined forces with the Channel Fleet three weeks later. Cornwallis ordered Nelson home to brief the Admiralty, and on 18 August Nelson's flagship *Victory* sailed into Portsmouth after more than two years at sea.

While his ships were being refitted Nelson consulted Lord Barham at the Admiralty, then went to Merton Place, for a brief respite before he returned to sea. He was exhausted, and needed time to recover his health. Still, his duty was clear. While Nelson was on shore Villeneuve slipped out of the Biscay ports, and headed south towards Cadiz, where Vice-Admiral Collingwood's blockading squadron was watching the Spanish port. Nelson was needed, and so on 13 September he said farewell to Emma and Merton, 'where I left behind all that I held dear in the world'. The following day he re-hoisted his flag in the *Victory*, and on 15 September he put to sea. He penned a letter to Emma, begging her to cheer up and adding, 'we will look forward to many happy years, and be surrounded by our children's children'. In fact, he would never see Emma again.

Nelson led his battered old fleet south again, and on 28 September he rendezvoused with Collingwood off Cadiz, which increased the size of his fleet to 32 ships-of-the-line. Nelson knew that these ships were at the peak of readiness for battle, and their crews were both well trained and eager. As his fleet lay off Cadiz he made sure his captains knew his battle plan, and would all do what was expected of them. He invited them to dinner on board *Victory* and used the opportunity to explain his tactics and his intentions. In a letter to Emma, Nelson wrote, 'When I came to explain to them "the Nelson touch" it was like an electric shock. Some shed tears, all approved… it was new, it was singular, it was simple.'

These captains, most of whom had never served with Nelson before, were encouraged to use their initiative, to be bold and aggressive, and to seek nothing less than the complete destruction of the enemy. He followed these dinners up with a written memorandum, issued on 9 October, which underlined this approach and outlined his plan to cut the enemy fleet into three sections, and destroy two of them. The novelty of this was that until Trafalgar, the line of battle had been an inviolable part of naval warfare. By abandoning it and opting for a twin thrust against the enemy line, Nelson was gambling everything in order to achieve a decisive result. He finished with his much-quoted line that 'no Captain can do very wrong if he places his ship alongside that of the enemy'. This was added, not so much as a tactical doctrine, but to ensure that even the least enterprising of his captains would play an active part in the close-range type of battle he was planning to fight. All that was left now was to encourage the enemy to come out and give battle.

In this patriotic but largely inaccurate scene set on 14 September 1805, Vice-Admiral Nelson is shown in Portsmouth, being rowed out to HMS *Victory*. The woman on the quayside probably represents Lady Hamilton, holding their illegitimate four-year-old daughter Horatia.

The battle of Trafalgar, 1805

The Allied fleet consisted of 18 French and 15 Spanish ships-of-the-line – 33 ships in total, supported by four frigates. While Villeneuve and Gravina outnumbered Nelson, the British had a distinct qualitative edge, so there was every chance the enemy would remain in port. While a lesser commander might be happy to blockade the enemy, Nelson wanted to bring about a battle – one that would utterly destroy the enemy fleet. Villeneuve had little desire to remain in Cadiz either, as thanks to Collingwood's blockade his food and supplies were almost non-existent. On 17 September Napoleon Bonaparte ordered him to break out into the Mediterranean, to land his troops at Naples, and then return to the safety of Toulon. Worse, Vice-Amiral Rosily was despatched to Cadiz to replace Villeneuve if he refused to put to sea. The French admiral had little choice but to prepare to sail, hoping to sneak past Nelson's blockaders in the night, or, at worst, fight his way to safety.

Nelson did everything he could to encourage Villeneuve. He took his fleet 50 miles to the west, leaving a handful of ships to maintain the blockade. This must have given Villeneuve the impression that he had a reasonable chance of escaping. On 18 October Villeneuve made his decision. He may have been prompted by reports that six British ships-of-the-line had been seen passing Gibraltar into the Mediterranean, possibly bound for the blockade of Cartagena. He thought Nelson's fleet had been weakened, while in fact these were ships sent to take on water and provisions, sent by Nelson in part to keep the size of his fleet down, and so to encourage Villeneuve to make his move.

He tried to leave harbour on 19 October, but light winds frustrated his efforts. It was the afternoon of 20 October when the entire Allied fleet reached the open sea, but it was disorganized as the Spanish were unused to sailing in formation. At around 4pm Villeneuve turned south, heading towards the Straits of Gibraltar. Halfway between Cadiz and Gibraltar lay Cape Trafalgar. Meanwhile Nelson's fleet had been loitering to the west, and when his frigates brought news that the enemy were coming out he gave the order that set his fleet in motion, steering a south-easterly course designed to intercept the Allies off Cape Trafalgar.

Captain Blackwood's frigates kept Nelson informed of Villeneuve's progress, and at dawn on 20 October, when Nelson found himself some 40 miles to the south of the Allies, he reversed course to the west. After all, he wanted to bring about a decisive battle, not encourage Villeneuve to run back into Cadiz. The signs were that the weather was deteriorating, and the approaching storm could give the enemy the chance to slip past him. He also wanted to come upon the enemy at dawn, rather than face the

The battle of Trafalgar, fought on 21 October 1805 was the most decisive naval battle of the age of sail, and one of the most hard fought. The majesty and destruction of the battle was perfectly captured by the 20th-century artist Harold Wyllie.

confusion of a night battle. During the early hours of 21 October Nelson altered course to the north-east, and as dawn broke he found the Allied fleet exactly where he expected them – strung out in a line to the east, heading south. When Villeneuve saw the British ships he ordered an immediate alteration of course, and his fleet wore round to the north. He planned to make a run for it back to Cadiz. It was too late. Before dawn Nelson had formed his fleet into line of battle, and was closing with the enemy as fast as the light breeze would allow.

Nelson was already on deck wearing his dress uniform, replete with his orders of the Bath and the Crescent, and the finery of an admiral. He was a highly visible figure, and would make a conspicuous target. His fleet was in two lines several miles to windward of the Allies, with the *Victory* (98) leading the more northerly line and Vice-Admiral Collingwood in the *Royal Sovereign* (98) leading the other. Nelson believed in leading from the front, but also these large first rates were the stoutest in the fleet, and best suited to soaking up the fire of the enemy during the long, slow approach to battle.

The Allied fleet was strung out in a long and vulnerable line, but Villeneuve also maintained a reserve, a force of a dozen ships-of-the-line under Teniente-General Gravina, positioned so they could reinforce any threatened section of the line. It was a sensible precaution, and it made Nelson's task all the harder. Still, Nelson was seeking to bring about a close-range mêlée, which would pin two-thirds of the enemy fleet in place. To him, this reserve simply added to the number of ships he would be able to engage. He relied on British seamanship and gunnery to do the rest.

Trafalgar has been described as a battle which was over before it began – one where Nelson's dispositions virtually guaranteed a decisive victory. In fact, his unorthodox tactics placed his fleet in jeopardy, at risk of being disabled before they could bring the enemy to battle. In 1811, the French tried the same tactic during a major frigate action off Lissa, and were defeated by British firepower. Nothing was certain, and to the men on board the leading British ships, being fired on without being able to fire back was a nerve-wracking experience. Those who survived the gruelling battle to come would also have questioned the view that victory was simply theirs for the taking. Instead they faced the hardest-fought and most blood-soaked naval action of the war.

This engraving by Thomas Sutherland captures the basic tactical situation at the start of the battle of Trafalgar. Until the two columns of British ships could break the Allied line, they were exposed to the full weight of enemy fire.

Nelson ordered Captain Hardy to steer towards the *Santisima Trinidad* (120), marking the boundary between the enemy vanguard and centre. Then, Villeneuve having hoisted his flag on the *Bucentaure* (80), he ordered Hardy to break the enemy line immediately astern of her. Meanwhile Collingwood was aiming for the gap between the enemy centre and the rear. Shortly

The battle of Trafalgar, 21 October 1805

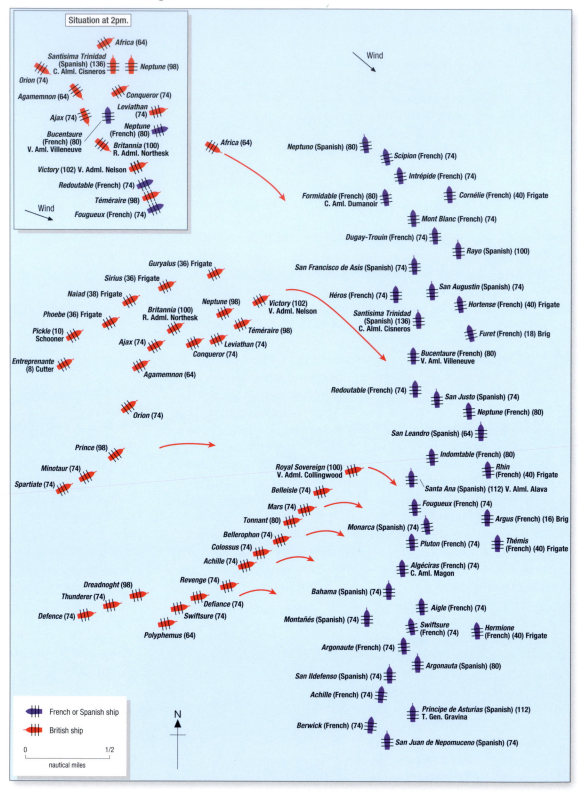

Situation at 2pm.

Africa (64)

Santisima Trinidad (Spanish) (136)
C. Alml. Cisneros

Neptune (98)

Orion (74)

Agamemnon (64)

Conqueror (74)

Leviathan (74)

Ajax (74)

Neptune (French) (80)

Bucentaure (French) (80)
V. Aml. Villeneuve

Britannia (100)
R. Adml. Northesk

Victory (102) V. Adml. Nelson

Redoutable (French) (74)

Téméraire (98)

Wind

Fougueux (French) (74)

Wind

Africa (64)

Neptuno (Spanish) (80)

Scipion (French) (74)

Intrépide (French) (74)

Cornélie (French) (40) Frigate

Formidable (French) (80)
C. Aml. Dumanoir

Mont Blanc (French) (74)

Dugay-Trouin (French) (74)

Rayo (Spanish) (100)

Guryalus (36) Frigate

San Francisco de Asis (Spanish) (74)

San Augustin (Spanish) (74)

Sirius (36) Frigate

Héros (French) (74)

Hortense (French) (40) Frigate

Naiad (38) Frigate

Britannia (100)
R. Adml. Northesk

Neptune (98)

Victory (102)
V. Adml. Nelson

Santisima Trinidad
(Spanish) (136)
C. Alml. Cisneros

Furet (French) (18) Brig

Phoebe (36) Frigate

Pickle (10)
Schooner

Ajax (74)

Téméraire (98)

Bucentaure (French) (80)
V. Aml. Villeneuve

Leviathan (74)

Conqueror (74)

Entreprenante
(8) Cutter

Agamemnon (64)

Redoutable (French) (74)

San Justo (Spanish) (74)

Neptune (French) (80)

Orion (74)

San Leandro (Spanish) (64)

Indomtable (French) (80)

Prince (98)

Rhin
(French) (40) Frigate

Minotaur (74)

Royal Sovereign (100)
V. Adml. Collingwood

Santa Ana (Spanish) (112) V. Alml. Alava

Spartiate (74)

Belleisle (74)

Fougueux (French) (74)

Mars (74)

Argus (French) (16) Brig

Tonnant (80)

Monarca (Spanish) (74)

Bellerophon (74)

Pluton (French) (74)

Thémis
(French) (40) Frigate

Colossus (74)

Achille (74)

Algéciras (French) (74)
C. Aml. Magon

Revenge (74)

Dreadnoght (98)

Bahama (Spanish) (74)

Aigle (French) (74)

Thunderer (74)

Defiance (74)

Swiftsure (74)

Montañés (Spanish) (74)

Swiftsure
(French) (74)

Hermione
(French) (40) Frigate

Defence (74)

Polyphemus (64)

Argonaute (French) (74)

Argonauta (Spanish) (80)

San Ildefonso (Spanish) (74)

Achille (French) (74)

Principe de Asturias (Spanish) (112)
T. Gen. Gravina

Berwick (French) (74)

San Juan de Nepomuceno (Spanish) (74)

French or Spanish ship

British ship

N

0   1/2

nautical miles

before the firing began, Nelson hoisted his famous signal – 'England expects that every man will do his duty'. It was designed as a boost to morale. His more important signal followed soon afterwards: signal 16 – 'Engage the enemy more closely'.

At 11.35am Villeneuve gave the order to open fire. By this stage the fleets were just over a mile apart. It took another 40 minutes for the *Royal Sovereign* to pierce the enemy line, between the Spanish *Santa Ana* (112) and the French *Fougeux* (74). She raked both the enemy ships and swung alongside the Spanish first rate, while the ships coming up astern of her widened the gap created in the Allied line. *Belleisle* (74) engaged the *Fougeux*, while the *Mars* (74) took on the Spanish *Monarca* (74). Over the next half hour the remainder of Collingwood's column entered the fray, battering their way through Villeneuve's rearguard, and pinning the bulk of Gravina's reserve.

At around 12.15pm the *Victory* reached the enemy line, exchanging broadsides with the *Santisima Trinidad* and the *Bucentaure* before piercing the Allied formation between the French flagship and the *Redoutable* (74). She raked both ships as she sailed through the gap, wreaking havoc on the gundecks of the French ships. The *Téméraire* (98) passed astern of *Redoutable*, between her and the French *Neptune* (80), while the British *Neptune* (98) followed the *Victory*, raking the stern of the *Bucentaure* as she slowly sailed past her. By 12.30pm the Allied line was pierced in two places, and Villeneuve's fleet chopped into three roughly equal segments. Given the light breeze, it would take time for the Allied vanguard to turn around and come to the rescue of the centre and rearguard. By that time – as Nelson had calculated – the British would have overpowered their opponents. The great gamble had paid off, and the battle entered a new and brutal phase – the close-range destruction of the Allied fleet.

The *Victory* might have broken the line, but she was now immobilized, locked alongside the *Redoutable*. The two ships pounded away at each other at point-blank range, while French sailors threw grenades onto the decks of the British flagship, and marksmen aimed at officers and gun captains. The bulk of the *Victory*'s 132 casualties were inflicted during this brutal hour of close combat. While the *Redoutable* suffered far more, particularly after the *Téméraire* (98) ranged alongside her starboard side, the open deck of the *Victory* was a particularly dangerous place to be. Nelson's work was done – he could do nothing more to influence the course of the battle, apart from waiting for the ultimate victory he now knew would come. He spent the time pacing the *Victory*'s quarterdeck, discussing the course of the battle with Captain

In this atmospheric but muddled depiction of the battle of Trafalgar at its height, a largely undamaged *Victory* is shown moving into position to rake the stern of the dismasted *Santisima Trinidad*. In reality, Nelson's flagship was locked in battle with *Redoutable*.

The battle of Trafalgar, 1805. This print by Robert Dodd shows the closing stages of the action, when, having failed to rescue the centre, the French van under Contre-Amiral Dumanoir fled from the battle.

Hardy. Then, at 1.15pm, Nelson was hit and fell to the deck.

The fatal musket shot was fired by a sharpshooter 70ft (20m) away, in the mizzentop of the *Redoutable*. The ball struck Nelson high in his left shoulder and smashed through his left shoulder blade, puncturing his lung and severing his spine before lodging beneath his right shoulder. Men rushed to the admiral's aid, and Hardy ordered him carried below. Before he went, Nelson told Hardy 'They have done for me at last – my backbone is shot through'. He was carried below, where the surgeon William Beatty did what he could in the charnel house of the cockpit, the makeshift surgery set up in the Victory's orlop deck. Nelson was stripped of his clothes and covered with a sheet. As the surgeon examined him Nelson accurately described his symptoms, including the regular pulsing of blood from his lung. It was clear the wound was fatal. As he lay dying, Nelson called for Hardy to give him an update on the course of the battle.

At around 2.30pm Hardy appeared, and Nelson asked him how things went. Hardy replied; 'Very well, my Lord. We have got 12 or 14 of the

HMS *Victory* breaks through the Allied line at the battle of Trafalgar, October 1805

Vice-Admiral Nelson had already worked out his battle plan long before he sighted the Allied fleet off Cape Trafalgar on the morning of 21 October. His fleet was divided into two lines, which would approach the enemy fleet at right angles, and break through at two points, thereby neatly dividing them into three groups. Rear-Admiral Collingwood in the *Royal Sovereign* led one line, and Nelson the other. At around 11.45am the French hoisted their colours, and for the first time Nelson could see which of the enemy ships served as Vice-Amiral Villeneuve's flagship. Despite having arranged a plan he was still able to improvise it, by altering course to starboard, thereby aiming at the French flagship *Bucentaure*. At the last moment he decided to pass by the stern of the *Bucentaure*, and push the *Victory* through the gap between her and the next ship in the enemy line, the *Redoutable*. The time was now approximately 12.30pm. As she broke through the line the *Victory* fired a broadside to both port and starboard, raking both the French ships at point-back range. A total of 1,148lb (520kg) of metal smashed into each of enemy ships, cutting their way down their long hulls, overturning guns, cutting men in two and causing utter mayhem in their closely packed gundecks. It was an impressive opening broadside, which Nelson followed up by ranging alongside the *Redoutable*, allowing the *Neptune* to follow behind him to repeat the deadly raking of the French flagship.

The battered remains of the Allied fleet at anchor off Cadiz, depicted after its sortie on 23 October when Contre-Amiral Cosma-Kerjulien attempted to recapture some of the British prizes. These French ships would remain trapped in Cadiz until their internment in 1808.

enemy's ships in our possession, but five of the van have tacked, and show an intention of bearing down on the *Victory*.' After Hardy assured him that none of his own ships had struck, Nelson asked that Lady Hamilton be given his hair as a keepsake. Hardy agreed, and went back on deck. He returned at around 4pm, repeating the claim that around 14 enemy ships had surrendered. Nelson replied, 'That is well, but I bargained for 20'. Finally, he asked Hardy not to throw his body overboard, to take care of Lady Hamilton, and, finally, he asked his Captain to kiss him goodbye. Nelson exclaimed, 'Now I am satisfied. Thank God I have done my duty.' Minutes later he was dead.

Back on deck Nelson's last great battle was drawing to a close. The Allied van had indeed tried to come to the rescue of the rest of the fleet, but it was driven off, with the loss of two ships. Contre-Amiral Dumanoir broke off the fight as too did Teniente-General Gravina, who extracted 11 battered ships from the great mêlée and fled towards Cadiz. The victory was complete, and Nelson had lived just long enough to learn just how stunning it had been. One French ship, the *Achille* (74) had blown up, and 17 more – eight French and nine Spanish – had surrendered. Dumanoir and the fatally injured Gravina had managed to escape with 15 ships-of-the-line, half of which had been in the largely unengaged vanguard.

Of the 17 British prizes, two – the *Santa Ana* (112) and the *Algéciras* (74) were recaptured by the Allies during a sortie from Cadiz on 23 October, as Collingwood was trying to save the battered prizes during a violent storm. Of these, seven were wrecked or foundered during the tempest and four more were deliberately scuttled. The remaining four were subsequently used by the British as floating hulks. Of the 15 ships that got away, four were captured on 4 November, and three more were wrecked during the storm. That left just eight ships-of-the-line from the great Allied fleet, four Spanish and four French. Together with the recaptured *Algéciras*, the Spanish eventually seized the surviving French ships in 1808 at the start of the Peninsular War. Few naval victories could have been more complete. Nelson had achieved his objective – the utter destruction of the enemy fleet. The tragedy of Trafalgar was that he died at the moment of his greatest triumph.

INSIDE NELSON'S MIND

On 12 September 1805, on Nelson's last visit to London, he visited the Colonial Office, and was ushered into a small anteroom. Its other occupant was General Sir Arthur Wellesley – the future Duke of Wellington, but then just an aristocratic and successful 'Indian general' turned colonial governor in search of a new command. Wellington later described the meeting between what would become Britain's two greatest military minds of the age:

> He could not have known who I was, but he entered at once into a conversation with me, if I can call it a conversation, for it was almost all on his side, and all about himself, and in, really, a style so vain and so silly as to surprise and almost disgust me.
>
> I suppose something that I happened to say may have made him guess that I was somebody, and he went out of the room for a moment, I have no doubt to ask the office keeper who I was, for when he came back he was altogether a different man, both in manner and matter. All that I thought a charlatan style had vanished, and he talked of the state of the country and of the aspect and probabilities of affairs on the Continent with a good sense, and a knowledge of subjects both at home and abroad that surprised me equally and more agreeably than the first part of our interview had done. In fact, he talked like an officer and a statesman.

Wellington later claimed, 'I don't know that I ever had a conversation that interested me more.' Few things sum up the two sides of Nelson's complex character than this incident, which took place just over five weeks before his death at Trafalgar. Nelson was certainly vain, pompous, self-promoting, sycophantic, arrogant and infused with an unshakeable belief in himself and his abilities. He could also be emotional, melodramatic and petulant. At the same time he was also the consummate professional, with an intuitive grasp of strategy, tactics and current affairs. When he wanted to he could be charming, and the clarity of thought with which he viewed these professional matters was matched by his ability to share his views with others. This duality lies at the core of Nelson's psyche, and for two centuries historians have struggled to understand the mind of Britain's greatest national hero.

At least one psychologist has blamed the more negative aspects of Nelson's character on his childhood, and the early death of his mother. Catherine Nelson (née Suckling) died when Horatio was nine, but as late as 1804 Nelson expressed his strong and lasting love for his mother, almost as if she had become an emotional crutch for him. As one of several siblings he probably

The real love of Nelson's life was Emma, Lady Hamilton (1765–1815), a former model, dancer and mistress who married the elderly Sir William Hamilton in 1791. She began her affair with Nelson seven years later, which continued until his death.

learned to seek his mother's attention, and this craving for recognition stayed with Nelson for the rest of his life, manifesting itself in his enthusiasm for the visible trappings of approval – the ribbons, medals, stars and titles that represented achievement and national acclaim. When General Sir John Moore saw Nelson wearing his full regalia he thought him 'more like a prince of the opera than the conqueror of the Nile'. The British public were more forgiving, and this ostentation did little to inhibit the heartfelt national adulation poured on Nelson after his victory at the Nile.

Nelson was clearly motivated by ambition, and so he went to great lengths to master his profession, but also to seek the support of those who could advance his interests. His almost sycophantic friendship with Prince William, Duke of Clarence, did him little good at court, as his father held the future king in low esteem, and therefore his friends were viewed with suspicion. However, Nelson also developed good relations with other superiors, including Earl St Vincent and Lord Barham. Even then, St Vincent felt that Nelson was better suited to command of a fleet than command of a ship, where the mundane duties of command would get in the way of his

Horatio Nelson enjoyed the visible trappings that followed in the wake of his victories. Here he is depicted wearing his Order of the Bath over an Ottoman Turkish decoration, the half-hidden Neapolitan Order of St Ferdinand and two victory medals, commemorating St Vincent and the Nile.

abilities as a dynamic admiral. Lord Keith was less supportive of Nelson, claiming with justification that, while in Naples and Sicily, Nelson had put his personal life ahead of his duty to the service.

Certainly his relationship with Emma, Lady Hamilton, did Nelson no favours. For a year this association dominated his life and career, and as a result his professional reputation suffered considerably. The scandal of his *ménage à trois* was the talk of society, and just as shocking was Nelson's shabby dismissal of his loyal but uninspiring wife Fanny. However great his abilities to lead men might be, he proved himself naïve and impulsive when it came to his private relationships. Lord Minto, the former British governor of Corsica, knew Nelson of old, and shortly before Trafalgar he said of the admiral, 'He is in many points a really great man, in others a baby.'

This said, Nelson's many faults can be largely overlooked, mainly because they were eclipsed by his spectacular successes as a naval commander. His heart might have been ruled by Emma, but the true passion of his life remained his sense of duty. For all his dalliance with Lady Hamilton, he spent much more time at sea than in her company, and as a leader his contemporaries saw him as nothing short of inspirational.

His 'band of brothers' – the senior commanders he relied on to secure his victories felt they were part of a brotherhood, and several, such as Captain

Hardy of the *Victory*, owed their status to Nelson's patronage. Nelson encouraged loyalty, but he also promoted independent thought, and his career was characterized by a willingness to act on his own initiative rather than meekly follow the orders of others. Nelson was equally adulated by the seamen under his command, who approved of his interest in their wellbeing and his ability to win.

Nelson was indeed a complex character, but for all his faults he had a host of good qualities, all of which played a part in his success. He could be charming, dynamic, loyal to subordinates, courageous to the point of recklessness and generous to his men. He was zealous in his duty, and had the ability to 'read a battle', to grasp the tactical situation and take advantage of it. His performance during the Trafalgar campaign also highlighted his ability to outguess his enemies and to fully understand the strategic complexities of a fast-moving naval campaign.

Above all, Nelson was driven by a strong patriotism, and by that almost spiritual belief in himself that first manifested itself when he was a fever-wracked teenager. In the end, this belief proved fully justified. With the possible exception of Robert Blake, no admiral in history could claim such a strong sense of dedication to the greater national good, or such a deep-seated determination to destroy the enemies of his country. Nelson was clearly no common being, and, more than any other, he earned Byron's description of him as 'Britannia's god of war'.

Nelson's 'band of brothers', the captains whom Nelson relied on to achieve his spectacular victories. Nelson made sure that these men understood his plans and shared his tactical doctrine. The plan on the table is of the battle of Trafalgar.

RIVAL ADMIRALS

During his career Nelson fought and defeated four fleet commanders, two French and two Spanish. He also fought against a Danish commodore, Johan Olfert Fischer (1747–1849), and a Spanish garrison commander, Commandant-General Don Antonio Gutierrez (1729–99), the latter being the only enemy commander to inflict anything approaching a serious defeat on Nelson. However, for the sake of brevity we need to ignore Fischer and Gutierrez, and concentrate on those rivals who held the command of a fleet.

Of the four fleet commanders, the unfortunate Teniente-General Don José de Córdoba y Ramos (1732–1815) was more accurately the opponent of Nelson's superior at the battle of Cape St Vincent, Admiral John Jervis (1735–1823). Nelson was merely the fifth most senior British officer at the

battle, and while he famously disregarded his orders to wrest a victory from a stalemate, Córdoba cannot be regarded as his rival. That leaves three fleet commanders, Vice-Amiral François-Paul Brueys d'Aigalliers, Comte de Brueys (1753–98), who fought Nelson at the battle of the Nile, Vice-Amiral Pierre-Charles-Jean-Baptiste-Silvestre de Villeneuve (1763–1806), and his Spanish counterpart at the battle of Trafalgar, Don Federico Carlos Gravina y Nápoli, (1756–1806).

Unusually for a French Revolutionary commander, Brueys was born an aristocrat, his family being minor nobility from Languedoc-Roussillon in the south of France. In 1768 the teenage Brueys joined the French Navy, and served as a volunteer in the Mediterranean before being selected as an officer candidate. He gained practical experience in both the Mediterranean and the Caribbean, and after 1780 saw active service as a lieutenant aboard the *Terrible* (74) during the campaigns fought in the West Indies during the American War of Independence. When the war ended Brueys was given command of a small sloop.

He returned to France on the eve of the revolution, and survived the purge of officers in the fleet, and the execution of the French nobility. In 1792 he was promoted to *capitaine* and given command of *Le Tricoleur* (74), only to be stripped of his command a year later and imprisoned on suspicion of being a royalist sympathizer. The French were desperately short of commanders, and as no evidence was forthcoming Brueys was released in 1795. The following year he was promoted to the rank of *contre-amiral* (rear-admiral).

From 1796 to 1798 Brueys commanded a small French squadron operating in the Adriatic, harrying Austrian shipping and supporting the land campaign of General Bonaparte. As a reward, Bonaparte requested that Brueys be placed in command of the fleet he was gathering to escort his Army of the Orient to Egypt. Therefore, despite his lack of command experience, on 1 August 1798 Brueys found himself in Aboukir Bay facing Nelson. His performance was lacklustre, largely due to his flawed dispositions and his general indecision. However, he fought bravely and died aboard his flagship.

Villeneuve was another scion of the minor French nobility, but he was an early supporter of the revolution and rejected his aristocratic roots. He joined the French Navy in 1778, but promotion was slow until after the outbreak of the revolution. He became a *capitaine* in 1793, but like Brueys he soon had his command stripped from him, pending an investigation into his loyalties. Also like Brueys, he was cleared, and promoted, this time to *contre-amiral*. He participated in the battle of the Nile (1798), but commanded the rear squadron, and so was able to escape from the debacle. He was captured by the British after the fall of Malta in September 1800, but released after the Peace of Amiens.

Above: Vice-Amiral the Comte de Brueys was a courageous naval commander, but one who lacked Nelson's wealth of experience and tactical good sense. As a result he paid for his shortcomings with his life, dying on board his flagship *L'Orient*, shortly before she blew up.

Villeneuve became a *vice-amiral* in May 1804, and that December he was given command of the French Mediterranean Fleet, based in Toulon. He never fully believed in Bonaparte's scheme to unite the French and Spanish fleets for an invasion of Britain, but his performance during the ensuing Trafalgar campaign was professional, evading Nelson, crossing and re-crossing the Atlantic, and fighting off Calder during the indecisive fleet action off Cape Finisterre. However, he never appeared to have a complete strategic grasp of the situation he found himself in, and consequently he never made the most of the few opportunities he was presented with. Instead he was left with one final decision – to put to sea and face Nelson, or to watch his fleet fall apart in Cadiz through lack of supplies.

It is to his credit that he elected to come out and fight, although his principal motive may well have been vanity, as he knew he was due to be relieved of his command. He also had little faith in his ability to win. Against an opponent like Nelson his ultimate defeat was a virtual certainty. After the capture of his flagship he was paroled by the British, and returned to France in 1806, only to die in Paris in suspicious circumstances. The official verdict was suicide, and consequently he was buried in an unmarked grave.

Finally, the Sicilian-born Spanish nobleman Don Federico Gravina also fought against the British during the American War of Independence, and was given his first command in 1780.

He participated in the siege of Gibraltar, and after a decade in active service he spent much of the 1790s supervising the much-needed overhaul of naval administration. In 1793 he served alongside the British against the Revolutionary French, but when Spain switched sides in 1804 he was appointed commander-in-chief of the Spanish Navy. Technically he outranked Villeneuve, but for all practical purposes the French commander controlled the entire Allied fleet during the Trafalgar campaign. During the battle of Trafalgar Gravina commanded the Allied reserve and fought with distinction, but was mortally wounded during the closing stages of the battle.

Above: The elegant commander of the Spanish fleet Teniente-General Don Federico Carlos Gravina emerged from the battle of Trafalgar with his reputation intact, but he was mortally wounded and eventually died from his wounds just over five months after the battle.

NELSON'S LEGACY

The whole process of celebration, deification and national pride began almost before the smoke of battle had cleared. Nelson's body was cleaned up and stored in a large barrel of brandy to preserve it on the long voyage home to Britain. The marine sentries guarding it were ostensibly there as an honour guard rather than to prevent the crew from pilfering the spirit. On 4 December the *Victory* arrived off Portsmouth, and then continued

Opposite: Vice-Amiral Villeneuve always seemed out of his depth during the Trafalgar campaign, although he had his moments, avoiding the trap Nelson set for him in the Mediterranean, and fighting off Calder's fleet off Finisterre.

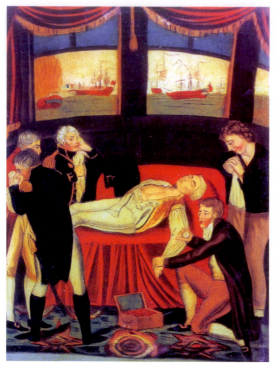

Above: 'Mourning the passing of Lord Nelson', a melodramatic and wholly unrealistic engraving, showing Nelson's death lying on a couch in his cabin, with the battle still raging through its stern windows. This seemed far more heroic than his death below decks.

Above Right: Nelson's funeral on 9 January 1806 was the most spectacular funerary cortège ever seen in London, and the Vice-Admiral's coffin was borne on an enormous carriage, pulled by six black horses, flying a white ensign at half mast.

on to the Nore, marking the mouth of the Thames Estuary. On 22 December the body was transferred to a yacht and taken to the Painted Hall in Greenwich, where it lay in state from 4 to 7 January, while tens of thousands filed past to pay their respects.

Nelson's state funeral on 8–9 January 1806 was a lavish pageant, involving a solemn procession of river barges from Greenwich to Whitehall, and then after an overnight lying in state in the Admiralty, the funeral proper began. The vast procession took so long to reach St Paul's Cathedral that the coffin had reached the cathedral before the last mourners had left the Admiralty. This mournful but splendid cortège was watched by crowds in inestimable numbers. Many were visibly weeping. London would see nothing like it until the funeral of Diana, Princess of Wales, over a century later, at least in terms of a visible public outpouring of grief.

The death of Nelson marked the beginning of the process of secular sanctification, as Nelson the sailor became Nelson the immortal hero. It began with Collingwood's initial dispatch, which described Nelson as 'A hero whose name will be immortal, and his memory ever dear to his country.' On 7 November news of his death broke in the newspapers, and the *Morning Post* picked up the sentiment; 'While we mourn at the fate of Britain's darling son, we have the consolation to reflect that he has closed his career of glory by a work which will place his name so high in the tablets of immortality that succeeding patriots can only gaze with enthusiasm.'

The lavish superlatives flowed on, matched only by a wealth of memorabilia, from popular prints to tankards, mourning rings and nautical souvenirs. It was understandable. Britain had just weathered the threat of invasion, and the country owed its national survival to the Royal Navy, and in no small part to Nelson himself. While before he was viewed as a national hero, and possibly a flawed one at that, now he was Nelson of immortal memory, the most elevated of Britain's pantheon of heroes.

The French, of course, were delighted. *Le Moniteur* played down the destruction of the French Fleet and proclaimed 'Nelson is no more', followed by a demand for an immediate invasion of the enemy's shores. Thanks to Nelson, such an invasion was now impossible. Other Europeans were more supportive. Samuel Taylor Coleridge was in Naples, and claimed that, once they perceived he was British, tearful Neapolitans came up to him in the street and offered their condolences. In the parts of Continental Europe where French tyranny was actively opposed, the sentiments were the same. The great victory of Trafalgar may have humiliated the French, but it was won at a terrible cost.

Artists soon played their part in the immortalization of Nelson. Sir Benjamin West's painting of *The death of Nelson* was viewed by thousands, despite the obvious absurdity of the crew of the *Victory* gathered round him at the height of the battle. Charles Turner's *The Battle of Trafalgar* focused on HMS *Victory*, which he sketched after her return to Britain. His earlier *The Battle of Trafalgar, as seen from the Mizzen shrouds of the Victory* was even more heroic, featuring the tiny figure of Nelson struck down beneath towering masts, as the fury of battle raged all around him. Finally Arthur Devis' emblematic *The Death of Nelson* dealt with the moment of death in the cockpit of the *Victory*, as Nelson slipped away into glorious immortality, surrounded by his devoted officers and men.

In 1843, Nelson's Column was completed, a towering plinth of granite surmounted by a 17ft-high (5m) statue carved by Edward Hodges Baily from Craigleith sandstone. Nelson gazes towards the Admiralty and Whitehall, and the sea beyond. The statue was finished off in 1867 by the addition of Sir Edwin Landseer's four bronze lions, adding that Imperial touch to an already spectacular national monument, set in the middle of the newly named Trafalgar Square.

In 1940, as part of the German invasion plan, a memo called for the removal of Nelson's Column to Berlin, as it was 'a symbol of British naval might and world domination'. More importantly, it was a highly visible symbol of national pride. Nelson's legacy and British pride had become intertwined. At the same time, Alexander Korda was filming *That Hamilton Woman* (1941), starring Laurence Olivier and Vivien Leigh. Aimed at an American audience, this new

Below: In this 19th-century engraving 'Saluting the Admiral', a bust of Nelson is honoured by a Greenwich pensioner, presumably a veteran of one of his battles. It sums up the way Nelson the national hero was venerated after his death.

depiction of Nelson at another time of national crisis was both a heartening romance and a stirring call to arms, as Nelson faced down the threat posed by an evil foreign dictator. The parallels between Bonaparte and Hitler were clear.

Nelson continued to evolve as a national figure, even though few can still recall more than his wounds, his love affair and his death in battle. In a recent BBC poll of the 100 greatest Britons, Nelson only ranked ninth, behind Princess Diana and John Lennon. While this might say a lot about the merits of such polls, it also demonstrates that some two centuries later the majority of the British public still regard Nelson as a great national hero.

The Royal Navy took Nelson to their heart. Warships were named after him, including the most powerful British battleship of World War II. Trafalgar Night is celebrated with relish, and Nelson is seen as the embodiment of the kind of naval professionalism that has made the Royal Navy such an effective fighting force for the past two centuries. The last word though, should go to the 'grateful citizens' who paid for the erection of that other Nelson Monument in Edinburgh. A plaque notes that the monument was erected in memory of Nelson 'Not to express their unavailing sorrow for his death, nor yet to celebrate this matchless glories of his life; but, by his noble example, to teach their sons to emulate what they admire, and, like him, when duty requires it, to die for their country.' There can be few fairer and more moving epitaphs than that.

Nelson's Column in London's Trafalgar Square was designed by the architect William Railton, and completed in 1847. The 152ft (46m) granite column was surmounted by a 17ft-high (5m) statue of Nelson, the work of the celebrated Victorian sculptor Edward Hodges Baily.

A LIFE IN WORDS

The business of celebrating the life of Horatio Nelson began almost immediately after his death in 1805. The first full-length 'official' biography of him was the *Life of Nelson* written by the Prince of Wales' chaplain the Reverend James Stainer Clarke and John McArthur, a naval historian and gifted biographer. The book was commissioned by the prince, and published in two slim volumes in 1809. By then his achievements had already been celebrated in countless broadsheets and newspaper articles. The business of elevating Nelson above lesser mortals began before Clarke and McArthur – they merely provided the public with what they wanted – an uncritical and hastily written 'official' portrayal of their great national hero.

A more edifying account was provided by Samuel Taylor Coleridge in his periodical *The Friend*, also written in 1809. He described Nelson as a man of genius, beloved by his men, and an inspiration to others. It was heady stuff, and the start of 'the immortal memory'. Coleridge's friend Lord Byron also added to this mythical aura by casting Nelson in a heroic mould in *Don Juan*, published in 1819. He described Nelson as 'Britannia's god of war', a sentiment which reflected the public need to sanctify their fallen commander. Another of Coleridge's friends, the historian Robert Southey, also produced his *Life of Nelson*, but this was an immeasurably better-written effort, and remains a highly readable and accurate portrayal of Nelson. Southey was prepared to expose the true Nelson, and while he was openly critical of his involvement in Neapolitan politics, and his affair with Lady Hamilton, it is clear that the author greatly admired Nelson and relied on the admiral's own energy, achievements and words to cast the subject in an altogether favourable light. Emma Hamilton hated the book, which of course may well have boosted sales, as it remained in print for several decades after the death of Nelson's mistress in 1815.

While other non-literary tributes followed – statues, paintings and the naming of streets and squares – no fresh study was able to rival Southey's biography. Writing in 1839, the Victorian historian Thomas Carlyle underlined the emphasis on the heroic qualities of Nelson. The Victorians continued to lionize Nelson. Thomas Pettigrew's *Life of Nelson* (1849) was typical of the studies produced in this era – largely uncritical of his private life, but following Southey's lead in casting Lady Hamilton as the villain.

The next serious and highly influential biography of Nelson appeared in 1886. Actually, Sir John Knox Laughton's *Letters and Despatches of Horatio, Viscount Nelson* was more of an autobiography, as it contained a well-edited selection of documents, gathered to form a historical narrative, almost as if in Nelson's own words. It therefore augmented a slightly earlier and less selective published selection of Nelson's correspondence, *The Dispatches and*

AN ACCOUNT OF THE VICTORY OVER THE
Combined Fleets
OF FRANCE AND SPAIN;
AND THE
DEATH of LORD NELSON.

Plymouth, Nov. 5, 1805.

Messrs. T. and W. EARLE and Co.
Gentlemen,

THE Pickle arrived here this morning—Captain Sykes of the Nautilas, went off express for London. On the 21st of October, the fleet under the command of LORD NELSON, consisting of 27 sail of the line, engaged the combined fleets off Cadiz, consisting of 33 sail of the line, *nineteen Line of Battle ships of the enemy, of the number of four flags, taken, one sunk, and one blown up.*

Villeneuve is board the Royal Sovereign: Gravina with 9 sail got back to Cadiz.

A gale of wind came on soon after the action, right on shore, and 'tis said that two sail which had struck, got back to Cadiz, that the large four-decker, Santissimo Trinidad, was in tow, but sunk; the Royal Sovereign, Victory, Revenge, Bellisle, Temeraire, Bellerophon, and Mars, suffered most. The Temeraire engaged two ships and took them, as did the Neptune two three-deckers, which struck to her. The Royal Sovereign, it is said, had 400 men killed.

Great as this victory has been, the country has to mourn the loss of LORD NELSON, who was killed by a Musket Ball in the breast from the tops of a three-decker, Santissima Trinidad, with whom the Victory was engaged, and actually lashed together. His Lordship was, at the moment he received his wound, expressing his delight at the conduct of his Second in Command Admiral Collingwood. Before he died, he made the signal, *that England expected every man would do his duty.* This, I understand, he was enabled to do, by having brought his telegraph signals to such perfection. We have also to lament the loss of Capts. Duff and Cook, and Lord Nelson's Secretary. Capt., Tyler wounded but not dangerously.

No other particulars of the loss have reached us. On the 24th, the Pickle and Donegal were at anchor off Cadiz, in charge of the captured ships. Six sail are said to have sunk.

I write in great haste,
And am yours, &c.

P. S. 'Tis said by some of the crew of the Pickle that they saw 14 sail in tow; the Nautilus is also arrived with duplicate dispatches.

Tasker, Printer.

The news of the stunning victory at Trafalgar was tempered by the death of Britain's most celebrated fighting admiral. In this contemporary handbill issued in Portsmouth on 5 November, the account of the battle is dominated by the account of his loss.

The 'immortal memory' of Horatio Nelson was honoured as a symbol of British martial prowess and national pride, although the manner of this veneration developed to suit each passing generation. Today, Nelson still remains one of Britain's most revered heroes.

Letters of Vice-Admiral Lord Viscount Nelson, compiled by Sir Nicholas Harris Nicolas, and published two years earlier. Nicolas had served in the Royal Navy during the Napoleonic Wars and so was well placed to select the most relevant documents. Together the two collections form a body of Nelson scholarship that have remained unmatched for more than a century.

By the centenary of Nelson's death the American naval theorist Alfred Mahan had cast Nelson as the admiral who established British control of the seas, and therefore an early believer in Mahan's own influential theory of sea power. Mahan's *Life of Nelson* (1884) was published at a time when the British took great pride in their fleet and its global dominance. The achievements of Nelson were therefore projected into a new imperial era.

While Nelson had biographers aplenty, it wasn't until the late 20th century that any of these added something new to our understanding of the man. Carola Oman's *Nelson* (1947) was a benchmark in that she used fresh scholarship to augment the much-used sources compiled during the previous century. As a result she was able to refute some of the myths surrounding Nelson, and painted a far more balanced picture of his troubled private life. Oman also challenged the Victorian view that Nelson had acted with singular impropriety in Naples by supporting a corrupt regime, encouraged by an unscrupulous mistress. Her efforts resulted in a far more human Nelson, and one whose achievements therefore seemed all the greater.

In more recent years Tom Pocock's *Horatio Nelson* (1987) became a popular best seller, perhaps encouraged by the jingoism surrounding the Royal Navy's part in the campaign to recover the Falkland Islands five years before. Christopher Hibbert's *Nelson: A Personal History* (1998) pushed forward the boundaries of Nelsonian scholarship even further by revealing new sources, while Colin White's *Nelson: The New Letters* (2005) went further, publishing numerous new documents which help explain the thinking that lay behind many of Nelson's strategic decisions.

The bicentennial of Nelson's death in 2005 led to several new books on the admiral, the most innovative of which were written by Marianne Czisnik, Andrew Lambert and John Sugden. Czisnik explored Nelson's psyche, Sugden used historical detective work to reveal hidden parts of Nelson's life, while Lambert unashamedly placed Nelson firmly back on the pedestal of 'immortal memory'. However, the most impressive study remains Roger Knight's *The Pursuit of Victory*, which draws on White's scholarship, but bases it in a historical context formed from a deep understanding of Nelson's navy. The result is perhaps the most thorough biography of this fascinating and complex character ever produced. Even here, Knight acknowledges that there still remains a great deal about Nelson and his campaigns that remain in the shadows, awaiting fresh scholarship to bring them into the light.

FURTHER READING

Adkin, Mark, *The Trafalgar Companion* Aurum Press: London, 2005

Blake, Nicholas, and Lawrence, Richard, *The Illustrated Companion to Nelson's Navy* Chatham Publishing: London, 1999

Clowes, Sir William Laird, *The Royal Navy: A History* Chatham Publishing: London, 1996

Czisnik, Marianne, *Horatio Nelson: A Controversial Hero* Hodder & Stoughton: London, 2005

Davies, David, *A Brief History of Fighting Ships: Ships of the Line and Napoleonic sea battles, 1793–1815* Constable & Robinson: London, 1996

Forester, C. S., *Nelson: A Biography* Morrison & Gibb: London, 1952

Fremont-Barnes, Gregory, *The Royal Navy, 1793–1815* Osprey Publishing Ltd: Oxford, 2007

Gardiner, Robert (ed.), *Nelson against Napoleon: From the Nile to Copenhagen, 1798–1801* Chatham Publishing: London, 1997

——, *The Campaign of Trafalgar, 1803–1805* Chatham Publishing: London, 1997

——, *Fleet, Battle and Blockade: The French Revolutionary War, 1793–1797* Chatham Publishing: London, 2001

Goodwin, Peter, *Men O'War: The Illustrated History of Life in Nelson's Navy* Carlton Books: London, 2003

Harris. David (ed), *The Nelson Almanac* Conway Maritime Press: London, 1998

Hibbert, Christopher, *Nelson: A Personal History* Viking: London, 1994

Howarth, David, *Trafalgar: The Nelson Touch* Collins: London, 1969

Howarth, David, and Stephen, *Nelson: The Immortal Memory* J. M. Dent & Sons: London, 1988

Kennedy, Ludovic, *Nelson's Band of Brothers* Odhams Press: London, 1951

Knight, Roger, *The Pursuit of Victory: The Life and Achievement of Horatio Nelson* Allen Lane: London, 2005

Konstam, Angus, *British Napoleonic Ship-of-the-Line* Osprey Publishing Ltd: Oxford, 2001

Lambert, Andrew, *Nelson: Britannia's God of War* Faber & Faber: London, 2004

Lavery, Brian, *Nelson's Navy: The Ships, Men and Organisation, 1793–1815* Conway Maritime Press: London, 1989

Lloyd, Christopher, *St. Vincent and Camperdown* Batsford: London, 1963

Oman, Carola, *Nelson* Hodder & Stoughton: London, 1967

Pivka, Otto von, *Navies of the Napoleonic Era* David & Charles: Newton Abbot, 1980

Pocock, Tom, *Young Nelson in the Americas* Harper Collins: London, 1980

——, *Horatio Nelson* Cassell: London, 1987

——, *Nelson's Women* André Deutsch: London, 1999

——, *Trafalgar: An Eyewitness History* The Folio Society: London, 2005

Pope, Dudley, *The Great Gamble: Nelson at Copenhagen* Littlehampton Book Services: London, 1972

Sugden, John, *Nelson: A Dream of Glory* Jonathan Cape: London, 2004

Tracy, Nicholas, *Nelson's Battles: The Art of Victory in the Age of Sail* Chatham Publishing: London, 1996

Tunstall, Brian, *Naval Warfare in the Age of Sail: the Evolution of Fighting Tactics, 1650–1815* Conway Maritime Press: London, 1990

Van der Merwe, Piete (ed.). *Nelson: An Illustrated History* National Maritime Museum: London, 1995

Warner, Oliver, *A Portrait of Lord Nelson* Chatto & Windus: London, 1958

——, *Trafalgar* Batsford: London, 1959

——, *The Battle of the Nile* Batsford: London, 1960

White, Colin, *Nelson: The New Letters* Boydell & Brewer: London, 2005

GLOSSARY

Beam (or Abeam) A direction at right angles to the direction of sailing.

Boat A small, undecked vessel, and a vessel too small to be described as a 'ship'. Often the term is used to describe ship's boats – the launches or longboats carried on board a man-of-war.

Bow The front part of the vessel.

Bowsprit A spar mounted in the bows of the ship, projecting out over the water.

Cable Either a thick, strong rope, often used to carry an anchor, or else a distance – 200 yards, or $\frac{1}{10}$th of a nautical mile.

Convoy A group of merchant ships, sailing together for protection and usually escorted by men-of-war.

Course The direction a ship is sailing in, usually measured in terms of points of the compass (e.g. north-west, south-south-east etc.).

Division	A sub-division of a fleet. Normally, the divisions were known as the van (or vanguard, the leading division), the centre and the rear.
Draught	The distance from the waterline to the keel of a vessel, and the minimum depth of water the vessel can float in without touching the seabed.
Fathom	A measurement of depth, equivalent to 6ft (2m).
Fleet	A large number of men-of-war sailing together, under a unified command.
Gundeck	The deck of a vessel where the majority of its guns are carried. Some ships-of-the-line had two or three gundecks – the Spanish *Santisima Trinidad* had four.
Leeward	The direction towards which the wind is blowing.
Line of battle	A group of warships in line ahead, or in single file, one behind the other. This formation permits the greatest possible number of guns to bear on the enemy.
Man-of-war	A commissioned warship
Mast	A vertical spar. Most frigates and ships-of-the-line had three masts – the foremast, mainmast and mizzen mast. These were formed from sections rather than one single spar, and therefore the mast was often divided into three sections – the lower mast, topmast and topgallant mast.
Orlop deck	The lowest deck of a vessel, usually located below the waterline.
Port (or larboard)	The left-hand side of a ship. During the Napoleonic period the word 'port' succeeded the earlier term of 'larboard'.
Quarterdeck	The part of the open deck of a ship behind the mainmast. Traditionally, this area was the preserve of the officers.
Rate	During this period, warships were divided into 'rates', graded by the number of guns they carried. For instance, a first rate carried 90 or more guns, a second rate 80–90 guns, and a third rate 70–80 guns.
Ship	A large three-masted vessel, with square-rigged sails.
Ship-of-the-line	A warship large enough to stand in a line of battle. Typically this would be a ship carrying 50 guns or more.
Squadron	A group of from two to six men-of-war, under a unified command. Several such squadrons might be grouped into a division (e.g. a van, centre or rear), or might form a fleet.
Starboard	The right-hand side of a vessel
Stern	The rear part of a vessel
Windward	The direction from which the wind is blowing

INDEX

References to illustrations are shown in **bold**. Colour plates have captions on the page in brackets.